THE URBAN ASIAN HOUSE

For my mother, Violet Mary Powell
with love and gratitude
and for Shantheni and Zara Shakira

First published in Great Britain in 1998 by
Thames and Hudson Ltd, London

British Library Cataloguing-in-Publication Data
A catalogue record for this book is available from the British Library

ISBN : 0-500-34162-1

Printed in Singapore by Tien Wah Press
Colour separation by Superskill Graphics Pte Ltd

Designed and produced by
Duet Design Pte Ltd

Photography by Robert Powell
with additional photography
in Singapore by Albert Lim Koon Seng, Peter Mealin
and Seow Cheong Heng
in Sri Lanka by Dominic Sansoni, Bertie Gunasekera,
Tan Hock Beng and Anura Ratnavibhushana
in Indonesia by Sardjono Sani and Oke Soetrisno
(Courtesy of LARAS Group)
in Malaysia by Frank Ling and Pilar Gonzalez-Herraiz
and Satoshi Asakawa
in Thailand by Todspol Tedrumpun and Ekarat Charoenpong
in the Philippines by Eduardo Calma

Preceding page: Aryasinha House, Sri Lanka
Overleaf: Eu House No. II, Singapore

ACKNOWLEDGEMENTS

A number of individuals have assisted in the research for this book on urban houses in tropical Asian cities. First and foremost I wish to acknowledge the continuing contribution of my secretary Lynda Lim who has typed eleven books for me over a period of twelve years. She has played a substantial part in the publication process, formatting and correcting initial drafts on each occasion.

In Sri Lanka I wish to acknowledge my indebtedness to Geoffrey Bawa, Anura Ratnavibhushana, C Anjalendran, Madhura Prematilleke and Hiranti Welandawe, and Channa Daswatte. Also to Rohan and Dulanjalee Jayakody, Lilani de Silva and Dominic and Nazreen Sansoni.

In Indonesia I received assistance from H Achmad Noerzaman, Tan Tjiang Ay, Sardjono Sani, Burhan Tjakra, Yori Antar, Ahmad Rida Soemardi, Witono Soetanto, Jaya Ibrahim, Made Wijaya, Zhou Fuyuan, Iwan Soetjipta, Budi Soetanto, Sonny Sutanto, Solichin Gunawan and Ani Isdiati. Erna Nur Eddin was enthusiastic about this new book and once again was generous with her time and the resources of the LARAS Group.

In Singapore I have benefited from the support of William Lim Siew Wai and Mok Wei Wei, Albert Lim Koon Seng, Tang Guan Bee, Chan Soo Khian, Ernesto Bedmar, Siew Man Kok, Tan Hock Beng, Kerry Hill, Justin Hill, Richard Ho Kong Fatt, Kevin Tan Ming Yew, Look Boon Gee, Tan Teck Kiam, Tan Kay Ngee and Alice Lem.

In Malaysia I was appreciative of the help of Jimmy C S Lim, Kevin Mark Low, Anthony Too, Lim Teng Ngiom, Saw Quee Jade, Lee Chor Wah, I-Wen Foo, and Frank Ling and Pilar Gonzalez-Herraiz.

Francisco Bobby Mañosa, Chelo Silayan Hofilena, Doris Magsaysay-Ho, Conrad T Onglao, Patis Tesoro, Vic Ampil, Gilda Cordero-Fernando, Wendy Fernando Regalado, Nina Quintos, Eduardo Calma, Rosario Ning Encarnacion Tan, Andy Locsin, Emmanuel Miñana, Jeffrey Isidro and Robert Borja gave me invaluable assistance in the Philippines, whilst Margie Logetta and Paulo G Alcazaren identified houses to be visited.

In Thailand I encountered the overwhelming hospitality of the people of Siam. I have to thank Theeraphon Niyom, Preecha Roogrujapaisal, Sinn Phonghanyudh, Chaiwat Wachpanich, Boonyanuj Chevakumjorn, Vira Impuntung, Nopadol Limwatanakul, Nithi Sthapitanonda, Duangrit Bunnag, Eakrit Pradistsuwana and Vittvat Charoenpong with a special thankyou for the generosity of Chirakorn Prasongkit, Bill Bensley and Jirachai.

Accompanying the photographs and text of each house are plans and sections. These are for architects valuable information for they convey the designers intentions and in the process raise the book above the level of the numerous 'style' books which dominate the popular bookshelves. For their assistance in redrawing many of the plans I wish to thank research assistants Foo Li Ching, Joan Lee Ling Mun and Chun Kian Chong.

Others who assisted in producing illustrations included Todspol Tedrumpun, Ramonchito P Olavydez and Dakshina and Jeffrey Fernando.

This is the third book that I have written on contemporary Asian Houses. In total 76 houses have been illustrated in the three volumes and they represent an extensive body of research and documentation of contemporary dwellings and lifestyle in Southeast Asia in the last two decades of the 20th century. For her continuous support in this endeavour I thank Lena Lim U Wen of Select Books Pte Ltd and Clara Pong. This book like the earlier two was designed by Ko Hui-Huy and June Lee of Duet Design. Shantheni and Zara have also made their incalculable contribution to the process.

- Robert Powell
Singapore

THE URBAN ASIAN HOUSE

LIVING IN TROPICAL CITIES

Robert Powell

CONTENTS

INTRODUCTION

'It is evident that in the rapid urbanisation of Asian cities, new urban patterns are emerging and new architectures also'

– Hasan-Uddin Khan[1]

According to a report by the World Bank, the world's population will double to 8.3 billion by the year 2025, with two thirds massed in cities and having more impact on the environment than ever before. The report produced jointly with the United Nations' Environment and Development Programme and the World Resources Institute gives a picture of life where the rate and pace of change means that humankind could have more impact on the earth's biological, geological and chemical systems during our lifetime than all preceding human generations (Reuters April 1996)[2].

There will be 20 Mega-cities in the World (defined as having populations of 10 million) at the turn of the century. Of these 11 will be in Asia including Bangkok, Jakarta, Yangon and Manila. Seven in every ten Asians will be living in congested cities with the attendant problems of pollution, crime, overcrowding and noise.

Creating livable urban environments in the city is therefore one of the key, perhaps *the* key challenge facing humankind. In this investigation of 'urban' houses in Asia I have identified twenty-three houses which indicate ways in which one might live with some dignity in the Asian city of the 21st century. My first inclination was to include only houses located within the dense urban fabric of city centres. This would have restricted the typologies to a range of row houses and courtyard house. But people fleeing the pollution and congestion of the inner city resort to life on the edge, in suburbia; this is also part of the urban phenomena.

In addition to terrace houses and courtyard houses semi-detached and detached houses are included, though, in a sense, they are inherently anti-urban forms.

The book is intended to provide clues for a *'civilised'* existence in Asia's fast growing mega-cities, without having to resort to the ubiquitous high-rise tower or slab block. It illustrates architect designed houses which reinterpret and transform vernacular solutions and others which indicate the pervasiveness of global culture.

I have purposefully included a number of houses which are built at relatively high plot ratios and which may be capable of being used as models for 'Living in the Tropical City'. Another consideration in selecting the houses for inclusion is the manner in which they deal with other concerns of those living in rapidly-growing, densely-populated Asian cities, namely:

- Pollution – dust, petrol fumes, noise and periodic 'haze' resulting from the burning of forests for commercial and agricultural development.
- Security – display of wealth versus the desire for privacy and the duality in planning that can result from this contradiction. In metropolitan areas around the world, theft and other crimes are on the increase. In several cities in Southeast Asia, enclaves for the wealthy have grown up (sometimes walled and protected by guards) where the affluent choose to live in relative security. Such upper-income enclaves occur in all Asian cities, but never far from the houses of the poor, for the rich need the poor as much as the poor need the rich.
- Access to work in cities such as Jakarta, Manila and Bangkok where, faced with two and three hour journeys to work on heavily congested roads an increasing number of people will choose to work from home. A common feature of several of the urban houses in the book is an office or studio with computer, fax, and Email facilities plugged into a global network.
- Humidity and rising ambient temperatures.

In the absence of vistas overlooking the Indian Ocean or the South China Sea and without the opportunity to exploit a close relationship with a rural setting, how then do we design? The urban house must do more with less. One method is by the careful choreography of space and natural light; framing internal views, to create illusion and surprise and variety on a limited stage. Often the most difficult site configuration challenges the architects ingenuity and produces an innovative solution. Examples in this book are The Jayakody House, The Stack House, Eu House No. II, The Windsor Park House and The Lem House.

I am also mindful that, to quote the Australian architect/ theatre designer Justin Hill, who lives in Singapore, "Every building has a night-and-day." The sun always sets early in the tropics and it is a magical time, for houses take on a different character in the evening when lights are turned on and the heat of the day dissipates. The verandah, the open-to-sky courtyard and, particularly the roof terrace, come into their own as an escape from the stress of city life.

In this book I investigate models for urban and suburban living in the increasingly dense urban morphologies that will become a way of life in tropical cities in the 21st century. It is a study of contemporary urban dwellings which continues the documentation of houses in Tropical Asia from the location where my last book *The Tropical Asian House* finished: at the *City Limits*[3].

The form of cities is not static and I have attempted to anticipate changing pattern. In Kuala Lumpur and Bangkok, two houses that are presently rural dwellings are included. One is the Dialogue House, designed by Frank Ling and Pilar Gonzalez-Herraiz, located at Bangi, south west of the capital of Malaysia. By the year 2020 the Malaysian government's intention is to build a new federal capital at Putrajaya, located in the so-called, Multimedia Super Corridor (MSC). The Dialogue House anticipates this urban expansion and the architects have designed it in such a way that it will eventually be part of a (sub)urban morphology.

Similarly, Baan Prabhawiwat is located some 40 kilometres outside Bangkok on the route to Pattaya. One would not immediately describe this as an urban location but when the elevated high speed highway joining the two cities is completed a linear conurbation will undoubtedly follow.

Urbanised nodes are being generated along the highway and the Prabhawiwat House is part of this urbanisation pattern.

Urban housing solutions can be summarised in a taxonomy of types:

THE ROW OR TERRACE HOUSE

Traditional examples in South and Southeast Asia are the Straits Settlement Shophouses that can be seen in Singapore and Kuala Lumpur. The emergence of the shophouse form which was widely adopted in Singapore in the 19th century and early 20th century was due to Sir Stamford Raffles having been Lieutenant-Governor presiding over British interests in Java between 1811 and 1816.

Raffles learned from first-hand experience that buildings unprotected from the intense heat of the sun and from the monsoon rain were impractical. Raffles would have observed that the Dutch used verandahs in Batavia. Some researchers have speculated that the shophouse was a fusion of the narrow fronted houses that are a familiar sight in Amsterdam with the shophouse of Southern China, especially Guangzhou and Fujian, with its internal courtyard.

Raffles instructions to the Town Committee in 1822, stated that, 'each house should have a uniform type of front each having a verandah of a certain depth, open at all times as a continued and covered passage on each side of the street'. Hence the, so-called 'five-foot way' came into being. It is an ambiguous space, sometimes cared for by the house-owner or tenant who will place plants and ornaments in the space as a token of 'ownership'. In other situations it will be neglected, the house owner adopting the attitude that since it is open to the public it is the responsibility of the statutory authority to repair and clean the space. Where shops open onto the five-foot way owners often colonise the space turning it into additional display area and some pedestrians volubly complain about this encroachment into the public arena.

The shophouse was a form that was adopted in other territories colonised by the British. It can be seen in Penang, in Malacca, in Kuala Lumpur and it has its equivalent in Jakarta, Bangkok and Manila.

Contemporary interpretations and transformations of the row house typology are included in this book. One is a Singapore shophouse, the Everton Road House, which has been extensively remodeled to accommodate a contemporary lifestyle. It incorporates a light well, traditionally used to bring daylight to the deep interior. Another example is of a shophouse which has been demolished and rebuilt, in the process revealing much about contemporary social aspirations and urban life.

Plot ratios achieved with this house form are high, commonly achieving 1.3:1 and offering the possibility of plot ratios in excess of 1.8:1. (Plot ratio (PR) or Floor Area Ratio (FAR) is the ratio of Gross Floor Area to Site Area and is a measure of the efficiency of landuse.) As an urban form, the shophouse offers many opportunities for transformation into contemporary dwellings.

Terrace house are also encountered in Colombo, at sometime under both British and Dutch colonial rule. The morphology is the result of laws defining the minimal size of permitted subdivision, which were introduced to cope with the traditional practice of land being subdivided and handed down to children, which if carried to a logical conclusion results in excessively small plots and overcrowding. Two houses in Colombo are included, the Lilani de Silva House and the Welandawe-Prematilleke House.

THE COURTYARD HOUSE

Traditional examples of the courtyard house can be found in the Philippines, in Sri Lanka and in Java. The immigrant Chinese brought with them models of courtyard houses which originated in the southern part of mainland China. The Dutch and Spanish colonisers also brought models of courtyard dwellings.

The Jayakody house in Colombo and the Contrast House in Jakarta are two contemporary examples which draw upon the long history of houses incorporating court-yards as a means of bringing light and ventilation to houses within a dense urban morphology.

THE DETACHED HOUSE

There are many traditional models of detached houses throughout South and Southeast Asia. The British, Dutch and Spanish colonisers also brought in models. Adaptation of these models to contemporary lifestyles can be found in Singapore, Kuala Lumpur and Manila.

The first European dwellings built in Singapore after Raffles' arrival in 1819 were simple timber shelters with atap roofs, but as the settlement became more established, perma-nent structures were erected. The founding of the colony was in the Regency period (1800-1830) and early houses built in the 19th century were symmetrical and compact and derived from country house precedence in Britain. Andrea Palladio's (1518-1580) restrained classicism was very influential and many houses followed the Italian custom with the *piano nobile* or main floor, at second-storey level (Lee 1968).

Asymmetrically planned residences began to appear from about 1890 onwards, influenced again by changes in European fashion. Asymmetrical planning created clear dis-tinctions in the functions and sizes of rooms (Lee 1989)[4].

Bungalows were popular in Singapore. The word "bun-galow" is derived from a Bengali word for an indigenous hut, the *bangla* or *bangala*. In its original form, it was a simple mud-walled structure raised about a metre to a metre and a half above the ground, encircled by a verandah. The British, adapted the original Indian form, retaining the front and rear verandahs whilst enclosing parts of the side verandah for bathrooms or dressing rooms. The raising of the house on brick piers or timber posts was an adaptation to the equato-rial climate, which, like the Malay house, permitted ventila-tion of the underside of the timber floors.

Although, strictly speaking, the word "bungalow" refers only to a single-storey building elevated above the ground, it has become common in Singapore to refer to all dwellings which sit in their own grounds as bungalows[5].

In the quaintly named 'Good-Class Bungalow Areas', Singapore Building Regulations insist upon 3 metre set-backs from the boundary on the sides of a plot and a 4.5 metre set back on the rear boundary. This has the effect of perpetuating endless suburban solutions. All detached houses in Singapore and Malaysia are to some extent affected by such regulations.

In the Philippines, Spanish colonisation precipitated urbanisation. The Spanish at first introduced stone houses similar to their houses in the Mediterranean but a series of earthquakes in the 17th century laid waste the Spanish colonial cities. The houses were prone to collapse and the colonists then looked to the wisdom of the indigenous house, the *Bahay kubo*, and merged it with the stone house. The second storey of such houses (and most homes were just two storeys high) was of timber supported on a timber structural frame which had some flexibility when subjected to seismic shocks. The first storey had a masonry wall which encircled the house but was independent of the timber structure. Thus was born the *Bahay na Bato* which was topped with an overhanging roof to give protection from sun and rain.

The first storey generally had few openings and relied on its mass to withstand seismic activity. The upper floor was lighter, punctuated by openings to provide cross-ventilation and the family occupied the upper rooms with the lower level being used for the carriage and later motor vehicle stor-age. Rosario Encarnacion Tan has designed a contemporary house in Quezon City which finds inspiration in the *Bahay kubo* and *Bahay na Bato*.[6]

THE SEMI-DETACHED OR SEMI-ATTACHED HOUSE

This house form shares a party wall with its neighbour. This is a model which also owes something to its popularity among British colonisers. I was born in a Semi-D (semi-detached house) in Britain. It was a house on an estate of perhaps 100 almost identical twins, all mirror images of each other. The quality of alikeness, sameness and uniformity were qualities found in their occupants who were almost all from the same socio-economic group. Any difference was expressed in the colour of a door or a modest conservatory attached to the rear of the house. The houses were in every sense a symbol of suburbia.

In Britain in the 1970's, a whole series of design guides were produced which gave acceptable rules for extending a semi-detached house. The rules were based on politeness and on good architectural manners. It was decreed that eaves should line through, windows should be of similar proportions and materials compatible. It was deemed impolite to build higher than ones 'twin'.

The manner in which one semi-detached house in Singapore ie. The Corfe Place House, has been rebuilt raises a number of questions about prevailing values in the suburbs of a rapidly developing tropical city in Asia. The house is located in Serangoon Gardens which is one of those private estates, on the outskirts of Singapore, that until the 1990's had changed little. It embodied many of the values of its counterpart in the English suburbs. It had resisted the rapid social and economic changes that had transformed the landscape since independence. But rising aspirations of the population, pressure on land, re-zoning at higher plot ratios and a commitment by government to give the population choice in housing inevitably reached Serangoon Gardens.

The house was formerly one half of an identical pair of Semi-D's. After demolition it was rebuilt and transformed to express, not conformity but *difference* and a breaking away from convention. The party wall has become not a common wall but a wall of separation, of demarcation, of defining one's own space. The deference of former times has given way to the assertive expression of one's individual identity.

Difference is expressed in the increased height of the house, which dwarfs its neighbour, and in the deliberate choice of a modern aesthetic that contrasts with the neighbour and materials that emphasis the break with the past. It is not unlike the Khoo House by Ken Lou Architects that was illustrated in *The Tropical Asian House* (Powell 1996).

THE EXTENDED HOUSE

This last category embraces houses that have grown and been adapted to the owners changing circumstances. Such houses intensify land use and often produce high floor areas ratios (plot ratios). They often grow by accretion for the best house plans have a robustness that permits change.

Four houses illustrate this typology. The house of Architect Jimmy Lim in Kuala Lumpur, for example, has been in a constant state of growth and change for some 20 years, while Geoffrey Bawa's house in Colombo grew to its present configuration by the amalgamation of four smaller plots.

Bawa's house is both his city home and his office. The house is magical. A city is condensed into a single dwelling: the street, the square, the piazza, the court, the outdoor dining space, the shaded seat beneath a tree, silent places, the processional route, the gentle splashing of water, glimpses of the sky, the reassuring hum of the distant traffic, music drifting from an unseen source, smells from the kitchen, distant views from the rooftop garden. Privacy is assured in this internalised environment and security is achieved by the high external walls and the relatively modest entrance facade.

In a similar manner, the Tesoro House in Manila has grown by accretion and the Fernando House in Manila has grown to accommodate an extended family.

THE GLOBALISATION OF ARCHITECTURE

"How far can the architect act as a mediator between local and global aspirations given the fundamental ambiguities that exist in Asian societies? The age of simultaneous realities is upon us, and their capacity to co-exist in an eclectic and sometimes syncretic manner is a positive trait. Many architects attempt to synthesise

the multiple strands of influence with varying degrees of success. There were early attempts to be local and "authentic", but we are now seeing the encompassing of many different influences, which has led to a wide degree of experimentation and ... (eclectic) expression in architecture."

- Hasan-Uddin Khan [7]

In the twenty-three houses illustrated there are diverse architectural responses to the processes of modernisation, industrialisation and urbanisation. Modernisation has proceeded at a faster pace in Singapore than for example in Sri Lanka or in the Philippines. Singapore's key position in relation to the globalisation of economies and it's geographical location has meant that its contemporary architecture has been exposed to greater penetration of contemporary influences than some of its neighbours. Sri Lanka has been held back in its modernisation by two decades of internal ethnic strife. The Philippines was severely hampered in the modernisation of its economy by the imposition of martial law in the 1970's and 1980's. There is a far greater reliance upon indigenous materials in the latter two countries, whereas in Singapore the technology employed is comparable with that found in industrialised nations.

An architect in Bangkok made a telling observation, that if one were to ask many people in the city where their homes are, they would probably answer Ayuthaya or Chiangmai. Not Bangkok which is where they live and work, but elsewhere[8]. I did not have the resources to test the extent of this sentiment but in Malaysia too, at certain times of the year, during festivals and public holidays there is a massive migration of people from the capital, Kuala Lumpur to their 'home'; an 'out-station' town or village. Perhaps this link to the vernacular explains the persistence of traditional forms in contemporary architecture in these two cities.

One would seldom find this sentiment expressed in Singapore. Traditional rural forms have been erased in the process of development, though urban forms such as the shophouse have survived albeit in a changed physical context which has often altered their meaning. There is in Singapore little apparent attachment to, or nostalgia for, past forms. The extent to which there is attachment to past forms is reflected in contemporary architecture in the megacities of Southeast Asia.

PRINCIPLES OF DESIGN IN THE TROPICAL MEGALOPOLIS

As I was concluding the research for this book in September and October of 1997 it was brought home to me starkly that a romantic or nostalgic view of the urban situation is not advisable. Farmers burning forest in Sumatra created, as they have done for several years, in the dry season that precedes the start of the monsoons, a dark cloud of wood smoke which was swept by winds north over Malaysia, Singapore and the southern islands of the Philippines. It persisted for more than two months. At one stage it was estimated that 100,000 hectares was blazing out of control in Indonesia. As the pollution index rose, the whole of peninsular Malaysia, Singapore and East Malaysia, and particularly the cities, experienced conditions which were hazardous to health.

In addition to this for the citizens of Manila, Jakarta and Bangkok the smell of petrol fumes and carbon monoxide is a daily experience and it is overpowering. A cloud of noxious haze often hang over these cities through which the sun barely penetrates. The idyllic tropical houses in my previous books inhabit a different world. In the absence of any progress in the control of these man-made disasters and urban pollution, to insist that houses in cities should not take advantage of air-conditioning would be unreasonable.

Cities are dangerous places too. Theft, kidnapping and assault are the dark side of urban living. One solution adopted by the wealthy is to create secure 'enclaves'. Another is to effect a policy of 'concealment' behind innocuous, unostentatious entrance gates which do not display wealth.

This sign of the breakdown and fragmentation of society perhaps portends worse conditions to come in Asian cities.

Forbes Park is one such exclusive enclave in central Manila. It is a beautiful haven, a calm oasis in a chaotic megalopolis of more than 10 million people. The enclave is typical of others in Bangkok, Kuala Lumpur, Singapore, Jakarta and Manila. This may be the way that those with material wealth will choose to live in the Mega-cities of Asia in the 21st century, with round-the-clock security and armed guards around the perimeter. One American academic has referred to this as "the return of the medieval fortress". It is one representation of the reality of life in the burgeoning cities of Asia .

CLIMATIC RESPONSE IN THE URBAN ASIAN HOUSE

In *The Tropical Asian House* (1996) I defined criteria for the design of dwellings in the tropics. A tropical house would thus:

- Have a living area which is the focus of the house and which is permanently open-to-the-sky.
- Not destroy any substantial trees on the site and be in harmony with nature.
- Be designed with the minimal use of glazing.
- Not have gutters.
- Be surrounded by a garden and non-reflective land-scaped surfaces.
- Have wide overhanging eaves to provide shade.
- Have in-between spaces in the form of courtyards, verandahs, terraces and shaded balconies.
- Have tall rooms to create air mass and consequential thermal insulation.
- Be naturally ventilated with permeable walls facing prevailing breezes or in the urban situation with air-movement induced by innovative design of openings.
- Where the site permits, be one-room deep with openings on opposite sides capable of being adjusted.

- Have duality in the planning arrangement to give openness and direct access to a garden or court on one side with a closed and exclusive appearance presented on its public face.
- Have air-conditioning in certain areas of the house e.g. bedrooms, to overcome the heat, noise, dust and pollution of the city.
- Make use of landscaping to modify the micro climate. Pools and fountains can contribute to the cooling of urban houses in addition to their sensory qualities.
- Embody the notion of *retreat* or *refuge* from the increasingly chaotic and polluted centres of Asia's conurbations.

How do the houses in this new book measure up to these criteria? Some reassessment of priorities is necessary. The desired openness of a tropical house which one can achieve in a rural setting needs to be balanced against the requirements for security and the need to exclude pollution, heat and humidity in the city. The best designs have flexibility in their arrangements so that it is possible to have both air-conditioning and natural ventilation. A minority of the house in the book have permanent open-to-sky living spaces but most can be opened up when the owner so desires.

The roof terrace becomes an invaluable asset as a space for retreat from the stress of city life. Eight out of ten city centre houses illustrated in this book have roof terraces. Hasan-Uddin Khan once described urban houses as 'fortresses of solitude'. The distant hum of traffic when one climbs to the roof terrace in the Jayakody House in Colombo is reassuring for the city-born owners. Rohan Jayakody confesses that he is not at ease in the relative isolation of the countryside.

Similarly, at the very top of the Ariyasinha House, also in Colombo, there is a secluded roof terrace, accessed by a narrow winding staircase, that gives a view over neighbouring trees to the distant lake surrounding the Parliament House. In the Goei House in Singapore the roof terrace permits the owner a magical view of the metropolis at night.

Landscape and water are an integral part of most of the houses. Almost all the houses illustrated have a pond, a fountain, or a pool which cools the interior but more importantly the sound of a small fountain, even a trickle of water, catches some primordial response in the human psyche, it calms and counteracts the stesses of city life.

Sri Lankan architect Anjalendran demonstrates a firm grasp of such poetics. He exploits the relationship between inside and outside and capitalises on the shifting patterns of sun and shadow, as all good designs in the tropics must do.

The courtyard in the Lilani de Silva House in Colombo is three storeys high and permits daylight to enter and for the sun to trace a path along the white wall of the living room. It gives an indication of the passage of time.

Likewise in the Dialogue House in Kuala Lumpur the overarching intention is through architecture to explore and rediscover space-time relationships and the ritual responses and events which emanate from these relationships. Ultimately the intention of the architects Frank Ling and Pilar Gonzalez-Herraiz is, "to reinvent realities and to discover new realities".

That it is possible to design house incorporating **all** the criteria that I have catalogued is illustrated by the wonderful houses of Geoffrey Bawa in Colombo and Jimmy Lim in Kuala Lumpur, which have grown by accretion over a number of years.

ARCHITECTURAL ISSUES:
AMBIGUOUS SPACE

The concepts of intermediary space and ambiguity are important keys to understanding the philosophy of symbiosis. In the West, dualisms are transcended through the dialectical method of resolving opposites on a higher level. The two opposites are either unified into a single entity, or one of the two is negated and rejected. Symbiosis instead creates a dynamic relationship between the two elements while allowing them to remain in opposition. A relationship between two opposing elements can be achieved by placing spatial distance (a neutral zone) or temporal distance (a cooling-off period) between them.
- Kisho Kurokawa[9]

There are theoretical issues which arise in parallel with cultural change in the cities of Asia. A number of houses reveal a conscious exploration of the so-called in-between space, with overlapping uses. The ambiguity of such space, is said to be a manifestation of the Asian way of thinking.

The focus of the Goei House in Singapore is a huge central atrium. It is as though the house has been turned inside-out and a public space introduced indoors, a sort of inversion. It could be a space for a street cafe, a stage, a 'theatre", a playground. The relationship of inside and outside and the interchangeability of the two is very much part of the design of this urban house in the tropics. Such ambiguities in the purpose of space have always existed in the shophouse form: the five-foot way is likewise a space, that is simultaneously part of the public and of the private realm. Ambiguities in the use of space are very much part of the post-modern discourse (Boyer 1996)[10].

The Dialogue House, located south of Kuala Lumpur, similarly develops this theme. The architects intention was to explore the incidental space, the space "in-between", the transitional space. The central atrium space in the Dialogue House is like a street, an almost public space, a fragment of the landscape coming into the house. Incidental, non-defined spaces will become defined or redefined by human activity and events, when the house is visited and inhabited. This area of ambiguity which writers, such as Kisho Kurakawa and Tay Kheng Soon, have pointed to as the essence of Asian thought processes, assumes much greater significance than in western architecture.

In the Tjakra House 'positive' geometric forms leave left-over or 'negative' spaces between them. It is these very spaces which become the area of maximum activity and energy. The entrance to the house and the principle staircase are located in this space. Sunlight, which amplifies and animates the interior also enters through roof lights in these, so-called, in-between spaces.

CONCEALMENT AND EXPOSURE

Other houses explore the often contradictory notions of transparency and enclosure, of exposure and concealment, individuality and anonymity, which are facets of life for urban dwellers.

The Everton Road House in Singapore provides a sophisticated and private lifestyle behind a suitably anonymous exterior facade that does not shout about wealth and status but integrates with its neighbours. It simultaneously speaks of exposure and concealment, of public and private, of transparency and opaqueness, of conformity and individuality: all aspects of urban life in Asia.

Similarly, in seeking privacy the three-storey Lem House in Singapore turns its back on its immediate neighbours. This is not an uncommon response in the suburban landscape of Singapore. A number of contemporary houses express 'difference' and 'individual identity' in this manner. But by its very transparency it opens itself to public scrutiny of the occupants and their lifestyle. It reflects a paradox of contemporary urban life where there is often a simultaneous desire for recognition and anonymity.

The notions of viewing and exposure are surfaced by the form of the Windsor Park House. The large amount of glass used for external walls gives the owner a panoramic view of the skyline of the city and of the neighbouring housing estate. Simultaneously the lifestyle of the household is exposed to view from these same neighbours. The living room is designed as a 'stage' surrounded by water upon which the 'performance' of daily life is enacted. It is almost a public space. One writer has suggested that the sloping glazing is symbolically a big movie screen and that the living platform

although public in nature, is surrounded by a body of water which reinforces the idea of detachment and solitude[11].

In the Carague House there is a overall feeling of transparency; the openness occurs behind an outer veil – the external high wall creating an intriguing duality. By its form it seeks recognition and individuality (a billboard) and simultaneously behind its external wall seeks anonymity.

THE HOUSE AS A PALIMPSEST: A REPOSITORY OF MEMORIES

The Lim House in Kuala Lumpur can be read as a palimpsest with layers of memory being evoked and where new meanings are constantly being inscribed and re-inscribed upon the text. Locked into the house are traces of the life and passions of the owners. There are diverse cultural references from Malaya, China and Australia, where Lim studied architecture: silk flowers, Chinese 'good luck' signs, dark antique Chinese furniture, *kopi tiam* furniture, vintage cars in various stages of maintenance and restoration, old safes, books, copper pots, red lanterns and pianos.

In the Encarnacion Tan House in Manila, the notion of a 'palimpsest' is strongly conveyed by the site: it reveals layers of family history and memory. Poetically, the top-most layer, the reinterpretation of a *bahay kubo* in bamboo which marks a return to indigenous materials, can be read as rising out of the ruins of a colonial heritage lying crumbled and decaying underfoot.

THE HOUSE AS A MICROCOSM OF THE CITY

The Lim House is analogous with a city in constant change and evolution. It is simultaneously a research centre, a resort, a residence, a workplace, a museum, a music academy, a resource library, a meditation centre, an antique shop, a garage, a restoration yard, an aviary, an observatory, an ancestral home and a temple.

There are a variety of moods in the house: quiet restful nooks and corners, formal and informal places, expansive semi-public places, a soaring atrium and precarious vertigo-inducing bridges.

In the Tjakra House the larger of two courtyards is an urban space, like a small 'public' plaza, enhanced by a koi pool, a tree, a timber 'park' bench. The elevations looking into this internal urban space employ a number of 'commercial' finishes. There is a striped canvas awning like a street cafe, corrugated metal cladding to the upper part of the facade and natural anodised aluminium sliding windows.

Likewise in Geoffrey Bawa's House it is as though a city has been condensed into a single dwelling. Metaphorically the corridors are streets and the open-to-sky courtyards and light wells are plazas. One experiences compression and expansion, deflection and anticipation, light and shade, silent places, fountains and trees.

The house is revealed as a 'city' of a myriad moods and experiences, of dark corners, of principle routes, of solitude, of gaiety, of exposure, of seclusion, of privacy and of public display. A city of visual and tactile details: a handrail, a painting, a bronze object, a door, a reflection, a derelict byway, roots of a tree, diffused light through a glass door and a drop in a pool. And a city of contrasting materials: wood parquet, cement, cobblestones and bricks. The house expresses at every turn the cycle of life with inevitable decay... and rebirth.

RETURN OF THE NATIVE

It is a mistake to regard the Post-Modern as a chaotic transitional period. The appearance of a highly differentiated architecture, the eruption of the evocation of new meanings is the manifestation of the architecture of the information age. The evocation of meaning through difference requires a keen sensitivity as an essential prerequisite.

– Kisho Kurokawa[12]

The majority of the twenty-three houses in this book have been designed by architects who have undergone part of their tertiary education in the USA, Europe or in Scandinavia or who have spent a considerable time working overseas before returning to their 'native' land.

It is arguably necessary to step outside a culture for a period in order to more thoroughly appreciate, be sensitive to and critical of it. In time, one would then be able to discard aspects of tradition which no longer have relevance. The 'returning native' brings a sharp perception of his (or her) own culture and with it the confidence to transform it.

Looking back at the previous two books that I have written, *The Asian House* (1993) and *The Tropical Asian House* (1996), it is apparent that a decade ago architects in South and Southeast Asia were struggling with the apparent paradox expressed by Paul Ricouer, " How to become modern and yet be rooted in ones own culture".[13] The houses in this book affirm that it is possible to be simultaneously Modern **and** to be rooted in ones own culture.

[1] Khan. Hasan-Uddin, Contemporary Asian Architects, Taschen, Cologne, 1995.

[2] Reuters, April 1996.

[3] Powell. Robert, The Tropical Asian House, Select Books, Singapore, 1996.

[4] Lee Kip Lin, The Singapore House, Times Editions, Singapore, 1997.

[5] Lee Kip Lin, ibid.

[6] Zialcita. Fernando. N. et al, Philippine Ancestral Houses, GCF Books, Philippines, 1980.

[7] Khan. Hasan-Uddin, in The Architecture of Housing, Aga Khan Award for Architecture, Geneva, 1990.

[8] Sinn Phonghanyudh of Plan Architects in conversation with the author, September,1997.

[9] Kurokawa. Kisho, Intercultural Architecture, Academy Editions, London, 1991.

[10] Boyer. Christine, The City of Collective Memory, MIT Press, 1994.

[11] Look Boon Gee, Singapore Architect, Vol 195/97, Singapore, 1997.

[12] Kurokawa. Kisho, Intercultural Architecture: The Philosophy of Symbiosis, Academy Editions, London, 1991.

[13] Ricouer. Paul, Universal Civilisation and National Cultures, in History and Truth, Evanston, 1966.

GOEI HOUSE

SINGAPORE 1997

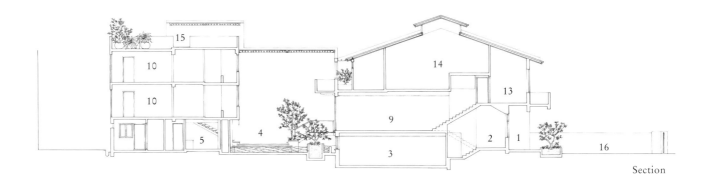

Section

Above: The idea of procession is juxtaposed over the layering of spaces. The entrance gate opens to an external verandah.
Opposite: The existing house on the site was demolished and a new house erected at a higher plot ratio which embodies the spirit, and yet is not a literal copy of the past.

The design for the house strives for tranquility and calmness. The design is inspired by the cultural and climatic nuances of it's context, integrating landscape, airwells and water features, blurring the distinction between interior and exterior.

The idea of procession is juxtaposed over the layering of spaces in plan. One's movement is choreographed to ascend, descend, move sideways and through tall sectional spaces, culminating in the open-air roof terrace. **CHAN SOO KHIAN**

The Goei House involves the rebuilding of an existing terrace house in the Emerald Hill Conservation Area. Architect Chan Soo Khian chose not to retain the existing facade or indeed any of the interior but has designed an entirely new house embodying the spirit but none of the physical structure of the past. Most architects confronted with this site would have lacked such convictions and would have retained something of the past, the facade perhaps or an existing airwell, the argument being, no doubt, that this would guarantee the authenticity of the adapted structure.

Whereas other houses in Emerald Hill such as The Tong House or the Helfer House favour accurate and, it must be said, beautiful *preservation* of the past (*Living Legacy* Powell 1994), Chan Soo Khian starts from clean slate. Everything is first erased and memory is invoked to recreate a new house that embodies the spirit of the past and yet is not a literal copy. In rebuilding the facade the architect has used proportions which relate to other buildings alongside but they are not copied.

The entrance to the house has a hierarchy of privacy which draws precedence from the traditional shophouse form. It was most often the case that one entered a reception room or a first storey shop and directly ahead would be a wall. Progress to the rear of the dwelling would not be along a central axis. Instead one would move either to right or left. Facing the entrance would be a

Above: An open-riser steel and timber staircase at the rear of the house gives access to a roof garden.
Opposite: The focus of the house is a large central atrium with limestone paving and a green tiled pool.

wall which would delay the view of the interior and satisfy basic *feng-shui* requirements.

Chan Soo Khian similarly delays the experience of the interior. There is a car park bay with a double width gate from the street, leading via a smaller gate to an external verandah. This in turn gives access to the entrance lobby. From the lobby one either moves to the right to ascend to the reception room, or to the left to descend to a basement studio/office.

The focus of 95 Emerald Hill is a huge central atrium, far larger than the traditional air-well. In fact it is like a public space, with two mature trees at the centre and a limestone platform surrounded by a green tiled pool with a weir introducing the sound of water. The space could accommodate a small pavement cafeteria. It could be a space for a party under the stars, a stage, a 'theatre", a playground. It is as though the house has been turned inside out and a public space introduced indoors, a sort of inversion. Such ambiguities in the purpose of space have always existed in the shophouse form. The five-foot way is a similarly ambiguous space, that is simultaneously part of the public and of the private realm. The relationship of inside and outside and the interchangeability of the two is very much part of the design of an urban house in the tropics. Such ambiguities in the use of space are also very much part of the post-modern discourse (Boyer 1996).

The house is divided into front and rear by the central atrium. The front of the house follows the profile of the gable roofs along the street and the interior

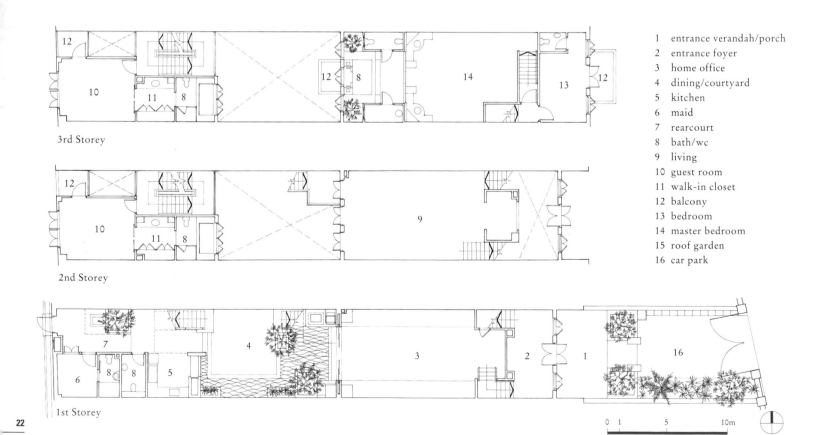

3rd Storey

2nd Storey

1st Storey

1 entrance verandah/porch
2 entrance foyer
3 home office
4 dining/courtyard
5 kitchen
6 maid
7 rearcourt
8 bath/wc
9 living
10 guest room
11 walk-in closet
12 balcony
13 bedroom
14 master bedroom
15 roof garden
16 car park

0 1   5   10m

makes references to the traditional shophouse with the insertion of stonework and timber fanlights above the living room doorways. The rear block assumes a more contemporary language with the introduction of an open steel and wood staircases, and flat trellised roofs. The front half has, above the basement studio and principal reception room, a double-height master bedroom suite with walk-in closets and a large jacuzzi set amid indoor landscaping and a second, smaller bedroom. The rear half has a kitchen and servant quarter and two self contained guest suites at second and third storey levels overlooking a second smaller airwell. There is access via a yard to a back lane. When first built many shophouses had no access from the rear but following the setting up of the Singapore Improvement Trust (SIT) in 1927 many back lanes were opened up and made mandatory for new terrace units.

The external naturally-ventilated staircase at the rear ascends to a roof garden. This roof terrace maximises the potential of space in the inner city. Climbing to the roof in the evening one has dramatic views of the city skyline and the distant hum of the commercial life accompanied by evening breezes.

The central atrium space is reminiscent of an earlier shophouse transformation done in 1984 by William Lim Associates, at No.102 Emerald Hill (*Innovative Architecture of Singapore*, Powell 1989). It was one of the first to explore the potential of the traditional shophouse for major internal remodelling and to critically question the perpetuation of a house form which was designed for a style of living of the 19th and early 20th century.

The atrium of the Goei House is covered by a steel and timber pergola which filters sunlight and cast shadows on the party walls. Above the pergola is an electrically-retractable glazed roof. The principle rooms look into this atrium and the three bedrooms have attached dressing rooms and bathrooms overlooking the central space. Behind fixed timber slats and sand-blasted glass one can bathe without being seen and yet simultaneously, unclothed, have a view of the atrium activities. A private life and a public life.

The ambiguity of such in-between space is a recurring theme in this book. The potential for dialogue between the two halves of the Goei House is similar to that found in the Dialogue House in Kuala Lumpur page 86. Kisho Kurokawa has pointed out the importance of the 'intermediate zone' in Asian thought processes and it's translation into built form where nature and building, exterior and interior can exist in symbiosis and opposing elements can co-exist in an ever-changing dynamic relationship (Kurokawa 1991).

The site area of the Goei House is 243 square metres and the built-up floor area 460 square metres giving a plot ratio of 1.9:1. The house demonstrates the potential of this model for building gracious houses in the inner city at high densities.

Opposite: The atrium is covered by a steel and timber pergola beneath an electrically retractable glass roof.
Above: The pergola filters sunlight into the central space.

LILANI DE SILVA HOUSE
COLOMBO 1996

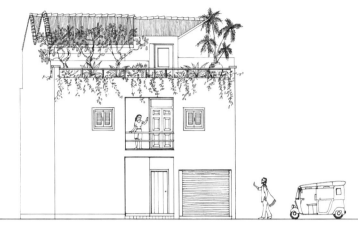

Elevation

.... the houses grew out of a feeling that there is enough time in the home that one can sit and talk where one feels like it, in a bedroom window, on the stairs, under a tree in the garden, not necessarily in a so-called sitting area. That one can sleep downstairs on the window sill or in a bed. That one has something beautiful to look at when raising one's eyes from the table, or that one sees something exciting from the living room – water that moves, or a seat under a tree – both contain a promise, and a temptation in one's thought to get up and go towards them... My own house was made so that one did not see a completed space – there was always a promise around the corner, the statue in a niche, the drama of going from high open space into a dark air-conditioned low cave, and the sound of water from a small pool that you could roll sideways into from bed. One could sleep upstairs or downstairs or out in the garden. The house is also a home for one's imagination – the senses become more awake by being used, and they get sharper... Buildings are also homes for our souls. *Ulrik Plesner in "Building for People", Sark fre Arkitectur (Denmark) No.3, 1971* – quoted by **C ANJALENDRAN 1997**

Above: The focus of the Lilani de Silva house is a sparkling blue pool strewn with flower blossoms. Opposite: In the late morning and early afternoon sunlight reflects from the surface of the water casting rippling patterns on the walls and ceiling.

The design principles of this urban house are rooted in the traditional urban morphology of Colombo. The long narrow urban site is surrounded by a high wall. This is a typical Colombo urban plot configuration. Building regulations permit site coverage up to 66%.

The site, 6.7 perches or 169.44 square metres in extent, is slightly broader at the entrance than at the rear. Like other Sri Lankan terrace houses of this type it is land-locked and cannot be serviced from the rear. This requires some ingenuity in the internal arrangements since the garage, the principal entrance for the owner and guests, and the service entrance are inevitably in close proximity.

Anjalendran solves this dilemma in a pragmatic manner. The kitchen and staff areas are located at the front of the house grouped around an open-to-sky service courtyard. A short corridor bypasses this emerging into the living area where one is greeted with a dazzling explosion of light.

Section

1 entrance
2 corridor
3 living
4 dining
5 courtyard lightwell
6 kitchen
7 maid
8 garage
9 preparation
10 bedroom
11 dressing room
12 bathroom/wc
13 guest room
14 laundry
15 roof terrance

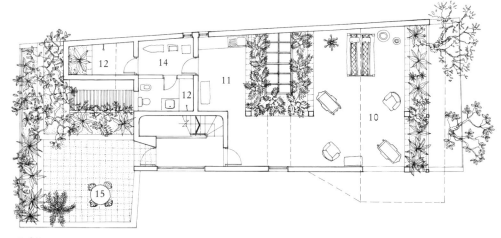

3rd Storey

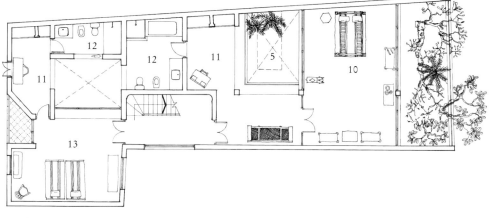

2nd Storey

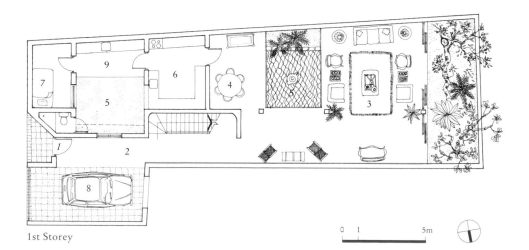

1st Storey

0 1 5m

Beyond the living room is a courtyard which extends to the rear boundary of the plot.

An open-to-sky lightwell permits light to filter into the interior.

A second open-to-sky courtyard permits light to filter into the interior. The focus of the house is a sparkling blue pool, with a tiny fountain, strewn with flower blossoms. In the late morning and early afternoon sunlight reflects from the pool creating a kaleidoscope of rippling patterns on the wall and ceiling. "Arrive between 11.00am and 2.00pm," instructs Anjalendran and he has coordinated the visit with appropriate music. At the rear of the living area is a third courtyard that extends to the rear site boundary (again the result of a building by-law). This courtyard is landscaped. The windows are thrown open and air is drawn through the house which has an openness in its plan arrangement and a feeling of lightness and airiness.

A minimalist cement rendered staircase with small diamond-shaped blue tile inserts gives access to the 2nd storey and two generous bedrooms which overlook the pool, each with the option of natural ventilation or air-conditioning.

The staircase ascends further to the 3rd storey and an extraordinary bedroom, open-to-sky on three sides. The owner may sleep here surrounded by the upper branches of trees .It is a development of ideas in the beautiful *Wickramasuriya House* (1993) which was illustrated in the book *The Tropical Asian House* (1996). A west facing roof garden invites the owner and her guests to retire to the roof in the evening to sit beneath the stars at tree top level.

The designer of the house, Anjalendran is a graduate of the Bartlett School of Architecture and he has been in independent practice for 15 years in Sri Lanka, having worked previously with Geoffrey Bawa. He is a prolific writer on the architecture of Sri Lanka and has been published in MIMAR and in Architecture + Design India. He also teaches on the Sri Lankan Institute of Architects architecture course, so that he brings an intellectual rigour to his work.

In this house and in others such as his earlier *House around a Mango Tree* (1985), and in his own more modestly scaled house, completed in 1993, at Battaramulla, Anjalendran demonstrates a firm grasp of the poetics of tropical houses in the Asian context. He choreographs spatial experience to make the most of a limited site area. He exploits the relationship between inside and outside, capitalises on the shifting patterns of sun and shadow, as all good designs in the tropics must do, and orchestrates views from the living area into the courtyard. The enchanting qualities of tropical rainfall are captured without the intrusion of walls or glazing. Breezes are induced by careful orientation and sizing of window openings.

Working with the climate and by the manipulation of spatial experience within a confined site, Anjalendran has produced another magical dwelling. It is a typology that could be replicated in other tropical cities (indeed it has some affinity with the traditional shophouse of the former Straits Settlements). The house has a gross floor area of 341 square metres giving a Plot Ratio of 2.01. Security is resolved in the design of the section and by the high surrounding walls. The owner Lilani de Silva has furnished the house with predominantly white furniture and several sensual paintings by George Keyt.

Above: At 3rd storey level there is an extraordinary bedroom, open-to-sky on three sides.
Bottom: A minimalist cement rendered staircase with small diamond-shaped blue tile inserts ascends to a roof terrace.

WELANDAWE-PREMATILLEKE HOUSE

COLOMBO 1992

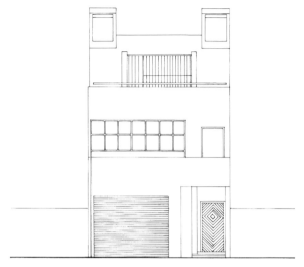

Elevation

The introverted nature of the house is signaled by the facade which is the antithesis of the traditional Sri Lankan urban house typology with open verandahs to the street. It reflects the changing social structure of the city.

The design of the house reflects the transformation of the Sri Lankan urban house in a changing physical and social context. The land is fragmented to a minimum plot size in a family tradition of land transfer where properties are subdivided among the children: a plot of 18 perches has been subdivided into three 6 perch plots with narrow frontage and long depth: a typical row house plot structure.

The house is introverted to maintain a sense of privacy in the heterogeneous social culture of the city. This is the very antithesis of the traditional Sri Lankan urban house typology with open verandahs to the street, and reflects the changing social structure of the city.

The design of the house reflects the lifestyle of the family: the family room is the centre of gravity of the house, visible from all parts of the house, to provide informal contact among the family members. The raised deck in the same room, approached by a ladder, provides for privacy while maintaining visual contact with the family room. The steel railing of the family room is finished with a wide wooden worktop which is intended to add a textural quality to an otherwise plain interior. This is a popular work area for the children and a welcome scene when entering the house.

The architecture of the house is modern and minimalist. However the manner in which the house relates to the outside space, the interlacing of the inside and the outside , was inspired by the vernacular house. As the central courtyard is a 3.5metre by 3.5 metre minimal space , this connection was achieved by relating it to several terraces placed at second and third storey levels. This stepped courtyard system creates a visual connection between the outside and the living room revealing a framed view of the sky. The east-west axis of the stepped courtyards adds a particular dynamism when the sun and moon rise pass over the courtyard in the in the heart of the house.

Shafts of daylight are used to punctuate the spaces in the house. The entrance corridor is dark with the exception of a pool of light created by a shaft of daylight cutting through the stepped terrace to the internal courtyard. The central courtyard is very slightly rotated anti-clockwise so that the corner column, bathed in daylight, becomes visible as one enters the

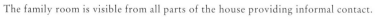
The family room is visible from all parts of the house providing informal contact.

Shafts of sunlight punctuate the spaces in the houses.

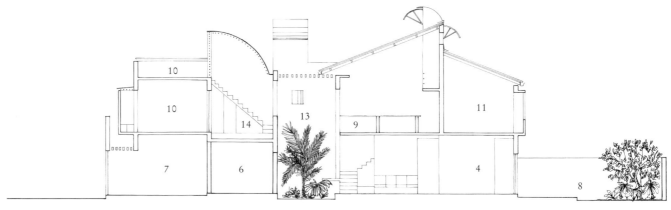

The wide lower treads of the staircase can be used as informal seating.

house. In the two childrens bedrooms wind scoops are used to induce an air current through the room. Each has a light-shaft to let in the rising sun, so that the rhythm of the household is set to the path of the sun. The light shaft also perform an important task in creating air currents for cross-ventilation. The varience of the path of the sun during the year adds a special dynamism to the quality of light in the house. **HIRANTI WELANDAWE**

Hiranti Welandawe and her husband Madhura Prematilleke both graduated as architects in Finland in 1981, and worked for one year with Balkrishna V Doshi and the Vastu Shilpa Foundation in Ahmedabad before returning to Finland to complete their Masters degrees. They made their way home to Sri Lanka in 1990 and set up Architrave Chartered Architects. They represent a young "returned" generation of Sri Lankan architects, driven by a strong social conscience, passionately devoted to producing a *modern* Sri Lankan architecture.

Their work is in a Modernism vein and both admit to the influence of Doshi and of Finnish late-modernism nurtured during their undergraduate training. In practice they divide the work in their office and each works independently. The best of their work is illustrated in their own house where they were able to decide how the house is lived in. In the design of the house they decided at the outset that it would be impossible for both to be the 'architect' and so Hiranti was the designer whilst Madhura played the role of client .

The size of the site is 6 perches or 151.74 square metres (a perch is equivalent to 25.29 square metres) and is the result of laws defining the minimal size of permitted subdivision, which were introduced to cope with the traditional practice of land being subdivided and handed down to children, which if carried to a logical conclusion results in excessively small plots and overcrowding in urban areas.

The house is entered from a narrow street and it is of modest proportions with a small yellow door alongside a standard steel garage door. Above the entrance is a canvas awning. It distinguishes the house and their eight year old son recognises that it is different to every other house in the street. Hiranti and Madhura jokingly admit that were it not for the awning the house could be mistaken for the garage of the larger adjoining house which is owned by

Hiranti's mother.

The garage occupies much of the street facade of the narrow house plot. There is no rear access lane to the house and this necessitates it being serviced from the front. The entrance lobby is in the form of a short corridor alongside the garage leading to a square courtyard, slightly rotated from the principal geometry, and thence to the living room. The courtyard is three storeys high and permits daylight to enter and for the sun to trace a path along the white wall of the living room. It gives an indication of the passage of time.

The living area is a double-height volume, overlooked by the family room at 2nd storey level. The opening up of this space between the first and second storey is intended to connect the children's activities with those of their parents. The detailing of stairs, handrails and balustrades is done in a minimalist aesthetic, which permits direct visual connections. The influence of Doshi, and to a lesser extent of Finnish late modernism, is discernible in this aesthetic.

Beyond the living room is a small, well-planned kitchen (The family does not employ a live-in maid) and a dining space which overlooks the rear garden courtyard required by building regulations in Sri Lanka for this house type. The built-up floor area on the first storey meets the mandatory requirement of being not more than 66% of the plot size. This is a high site coverage compared with

The rhythm of the house is set to the path of the sun.

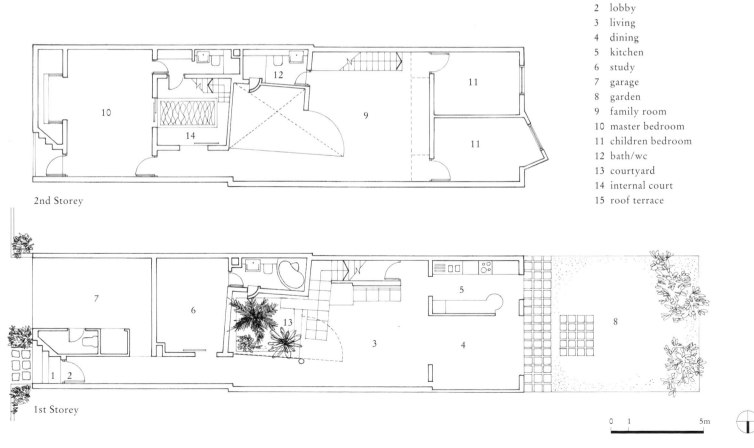

1 entrance
2 lobby
3 living
4 dining
5 kitchen
6 study
7 garage
8 garden
9 family room
10 master bedroom
11 children bedroom
12 bath/wc
13 courtyard
14 internal court
15 roof terrace

2nd Storey

1st Storey

0 1   5m

Top and above: At 2nd storey level the principle rooms are arranged around the stepped courtyard.

many house types in Asian cities.

At second storey level the principle rooms are arranged around the light well above the garden court. Looking upwards from the garden court a delightful space is revealed. Outside the master bedroom is a terrace with a shallow rectangular pool. A concrete stair visible from the living room leads upwards from this terrace to the roof garden above the master bedroom. The wall flanking the stair is painted bright orange, an iscolated splash of colour in the predominantly monochrome house.

The roof garden is wonderful. Before dinner their guests converse under a clear starlit sky in bright moonlight. In the frequent power cuts that Colombo experienced in 1996 it performed a much more utilitarian function; the family moved their mattresses onto the roof and slept under the stars.

This is a delightful house and a lucid example of a modernist aesthetic which simultaneously builds upon the attributes of a traditional typology.

Both Hiranti and Madhura are teachers in addition to being practitioners. One at the University of Moratuwa, the other at the Sri Lankan Institute of Architects which has a course that is more practice based. They are critical of the so-called 'umbrella aesthetic' in Sri Lanka which to quote Madhura, "Carries with it an idealisation of rural life, usually feudal rural life. This ideology generates architectural models with an inherent anti-urban bias. This prejudice is responsible for the lack of urbanity in our city."[2]

Madhura has also criticised, "the widespread practice in the name of 're-cycling,' of scavenging and destroying valuable old buildings and even entire streets so that we may lean on the glory of the stolen columns."[3]

The restraint exercised in their own house is less evident in later houses they have designed. The shifting geometry in some of these other houses speaks perhaps of the dislocation felt in a city with constant roadblocks and disruption. There is an air of tension in Colombo, with soldiers at every other street corner, in a state of nervous alertness, juxtaposed against an atmosphere of total normality as people go about their daily routine. Later designs of both Welandawe and Prematilleke reflect that state of fragmentation in urban life.

[1] Powell, Robert. *The Tropical Asian House*, Select Books, Singapore, 1996 (Reprinted 1997).
[2] Prematilleke. Madhura, 'Beyond the Umbrella and other Stories', Annual Session of the Sri Lanka Institute of Architects, February 1997.
[3] Ibid.

An external stair ascends to the roof terrace above the master bedroom.

EVERTON ROAD HOUSE

SINGAPORE 1995

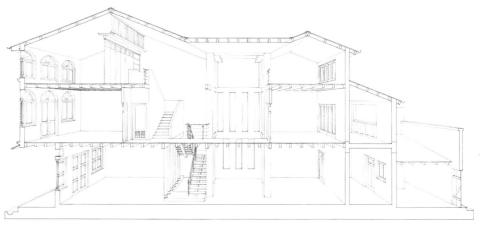

Section

Inner city living in a shophouse configuration has it's limitations, for example, the lack of greenery, but that does not prevent one from imbuing a sense of tranquility within the walls – a sort of sanctuary from the hustle and bustle of city life – an environment to contemplate one's condition in this fast-paced technology-driven city life. That is my intent whenever I set out to craft an urban house. **RICHARD HO**

The five-foot way, a continuous covered walkway, fronting the shophouses in Everton Road is a legacy of Sir Stamford Raffles who in 1822 issued instructions on the layout of the Singapore settlement.

The Everton Road House involves the internal transformation of an early 20th century shophouse into a contemporary urban dwelling.

Architect Richard Ho adopts an unwavering attitude to conservation of shophouses maintaining that their conservation should not be narrowly defined as replication or preservation. Present conservation guidelines in Singapore strictly control the exterior of the shophouse, even on completely new extensions to the extent that the type and size of openings and even materials are limited-measures which Richard Ho decries as over restrictive.

Hence while the exterior of the shophouse and the five-foot way are retained and maintain the scale and character of the street, the interior of the building has undergone a dramatic transformation to accommodate new spatial and functional requirements. Unlike national monuments where an argument can be made for preservation the shophouse lends itself to sensitive adaptation to meet the needs of contemporary society.

The central airwell that characterises most shophouses is retained but it is dramatised far beyond its original utilitarian purpose. Whereas formerly such air wells brought minimal light and ventilation to the gloomy interior, in the Everton Road House the lightwell becomes a 'lantern', a glazed cube that slices through the centre of the plan to bring daylight flooding into the core of the house during the day. At night the lantern is illuminated by spotlights placed in niches in the party wall.

Conservation guidelines strictly control the street facades in Singapore's conservation districts. The external facade reveals little of the lifestyle of the occupants.

1 five-foot way
2 living
3 stairwell
4 dining
5 airwell/lightwell
6 kitchen
7 bathroom
8 utility
9 study
10 bedroom
11 terrace

Above: The staircase orchestrates experiences of the transformed spatial quality.

Opposite: Dramatic changes have been made to the internal spatial quality. The notion of transparency is explored with the opening-up of the shophouse interior.

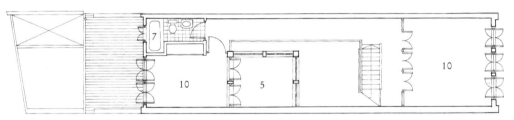

3rd Storey

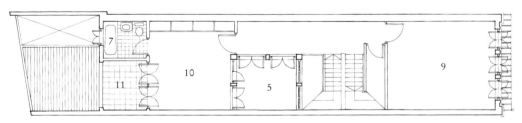

2nd Storey

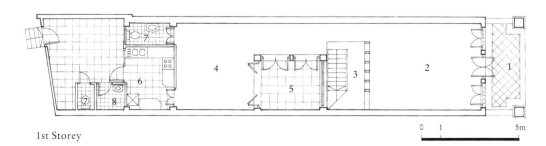

1st Storey

0   1   5m

The staircase, traditionally an element which was downplayed and strictly functional, in this case is dramatised as it ascends first alongside the lantern and then at right angles to it opening up a space through three storeys of the house. All the major rooms of the house have a view into this space and at second storey level a gallery runs alongside it connecting the front and rear of the house. Likewise at third storey level a light-weight timber bridge creates a connection.

The notion of transparency is explored with the opening up of the interior that is the antithesis of the spatial qualities of the original shophouse. The wall which traditionally blocked the immediate view of the interior is dematerialised, becoming an open system of display shelves. The interior spaces are layered with a general feeling of lightness and clarity in the studied juxtaposition of vertical and horizontal elements .

A combination of natural timber and muted yellow ochre and white adds to this clarity. Floors are yellow Vietnamese tiles and the external wall of the 'lantern' is a smooth textured Sienna yellow.

Originally designed for use by a family, the house has been rented, and it has proven adaptable to the needs of an expatriate businessman, within minutes of the Central Business District and entertainment facilities; with space for display of art works, a home-office space, for overnight guests and with internal spaces that make it a potentially wonderful place for parties.

The conservation of the Everton Road House shows the ability of such structures to be adapted to meet the requirements of contemporary living. It provides for a sophisticated and private lifestyle behind a suitably anonymous exterior facade that does not shout about wealth and status but integrates with its neighbours. It simultaneously speaks of exposure and concealment, of public and private, of transparency and opaqueness, of conformity and individuality: all aspects of urban life in Asia.

In the process Richard Ho and assistant architect Lee Song-Wee have demonstrated the continuing ability of the shophouse form to satisfy the housing needs of the contemporary urban dweller. It provides inspiration for new urban housing in Asia's fast growing cities for on the site area of 115 square metres, 302 square metres of floor space is provided giving a Plot Ratio of 2.6:1. This plot ratio is comparable with the adjacent high-rise residential towers and the house has a much more immediate relationship with the 'street' than experienced by apartment dwellers.

Above: The staircase, traditionally an element which was downplayed, is dramatised as it ascends alongside the lightwell.
Opposite: Daylight floods into the heart of the house. At night the lightwell is illuminated by spotlights.

STACK HOUSE

THE COURTYARD HOUSE
ARCHITECT: **ACHMAD NOERZAMAN
AND ARIESWARI P PUTRI
• ARKONIN**

Above: Entering the house one encounters a reception area. At a slightly higher level is the living area and a sunlit courtyard with a tiny waterfall

Opposite: The house which is located at the turning point of the street acts as a modest landmark.

The Stack House is located in an established neighbourhood of Jakarta with an existing morphological pattern of one- and two-storey terrace houses. The site of the house is an awkward triangular shaped site at a bend in the road with a narrow frontage of 5.26 metres, widening to the rear. Typical of an urban site in Java, the neighbours have built right to the boundary so that the site boundary is high solid walls with no view out other than to the street. The architects solution is ingenious and turns these disadvantages to good effect by the use of two internal courtyards. Air movement is assisted by these two courtyards, one of them being adjacent to the living space. In this courtyard is a tiny waterfall which tumbles down the rear wall drowning the extraneous noises of the neighbourhood. The sound of water soothes and calms the spirits. The second courtyard serves to ventilate the service areas.

The *parti* is two overlapping geometric shapes, a rectangle and a parallelogram aligned with the boundaries of the site. This creates an in-between space at the heart of the plan which is projected upwards to give a soaring internal two-and-a-half storey high atrium which assists in the upward movement of air. Sunlight penetrates through a circular glazed roof light and moves like a sundial across the room. The movement of sunlight across the curved yellow wall is delightful in the late afternoon and evening. The name 'Stack' house comes from the architect's stacking of accommodation with overlapping uses. It also refers to the 'Stack' effect of ventilation.

All major rooms face the street with a variety of opening windows to induce cross-ventilation. On such a tight site with such a narrow street frontage, it was always going to be a problem to achieve natural daylight and ventilation. The fact that it is done here with very little evidence of difficulty suggests this is an exemplary plan.

The house has a basement garage and a loft which has been turned into a secluded work space. When windows are opened in the loft, it further assists in the movement of air through the house.

The house has the overlapping uses and ambiguous boundaries of a traditional Indonesian house. It also incorporates religious rituals. A wall at second storey level is placed with the intention of defining the *quibla*, the direction to

The curved wall of the *mushalla* or prayer room at 2nd storey level indicates the direction of Mecca.

1 entrance
2 reception
3 living room
4 dining
5 courtyard
6 pantry
7 master bedroom
8 bathroom/wc
9 musholla–prayer room
10 play area
11 bedroom
12 maid
13 service area
14 terrace
15 garage
16 studio

0   1   5m

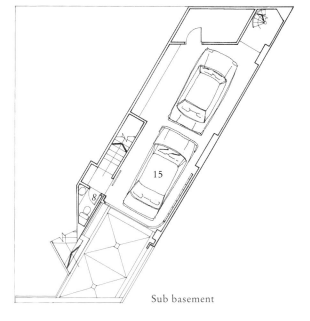

Sub basement

Mecca, in a space adopted as the Muslim *Musholla* or prayer room. There is a hierarchy of privacy similar to that found in traditional dwellings. Just inside the entrance is a space for greeting guests. There are then steps up to the more private family, living area and dining area. Boundaries are thus subtly defined.

The site area is just 145 m² and the built up floor area 255 square metres giving a plot ratio of 1.75:1. With a site coverage of 70.3% this is a highly efficient use of urban land. It is a brilliant solution for a town house for a small family with a live-in maid. It gives an impression of spaciousness despite being very small, though some sense of *enclosure* is inevitable.

Noerzaman and his wife Arieswari, both graduates from the University of Indonesia, School of Architecture, wanted a house that was easy to run and needed relatively little maintenance, also a house that would use relatively few natural resources. Even without air-conditioning, it is cool. The design of top hung windows, sliding doors, balconies and courtyards is fundamental to this strategy. The house fulfills the basic premise of a house in the tropics. The living area opens directly to open air (the court) and it is naturally ventilated (except in the case of the bedrooms). The Venturi effect is employed. The location of the two smaller courtyards in the deepest extremes of the site assists in this regard.

The house stands out from, but does not dominate, the smaller neighbouring houses. It adds to the spatial quality of the street by defining the turning point. It acts as a significant though modest urban landmark.

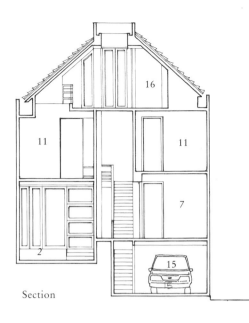

Section

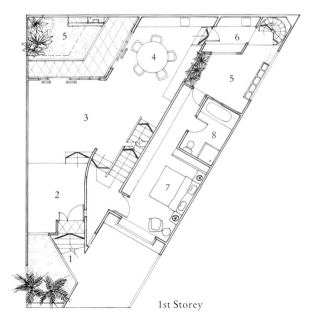

1st Storey

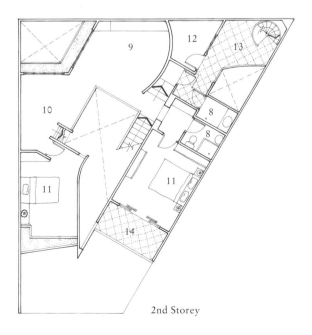

2nd Storey

Opposite: The soaring atrium space at the centre of the house creates a 'stack' effect which assists in the vertical movement of air.

Above: Sunlight penetrates through a circular rooflight at the very heart of the plan and moves like a sundial across the house. An almost vertical stair gives access to the attic studio.

JAYAKODY HOUSE

COLOMBO 1995

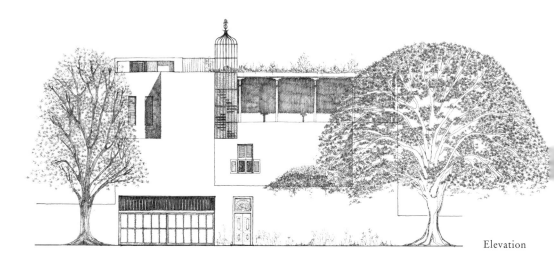

Elevation

The street elevation is modest and restrained.

The Jayakody house is simply stunning. The awkward configuration of the site had caused it to be rejected by numerous potential buyers and their architects but its potential was immediately grasped by Bawa. The result is a house of immense peace and serenity in a city which has visible signs of underlying tensions.

Hasan-Uddin Khan once described urban houses as 'fortresses of solitude'.[1] This description would fit the Jayakody House perfectly. The distant hum of traffic when one climbs to the roof terrace is reassuring for the city-born owners. Rohan Jayakody confesses that he is not at ease in the relative isolation of the countryside.

Within the house there are moments of immense stillness. The slow movement of the sun across the courtyard wall is magical. A measure of the passing of time it reminds one of the serenity of the garden of the Palazzo Querina Stampalia in Venice designed by Carlo Scarpa. One is reminded too of a description of Scarpa's work; that he had the ability to create architecture that was simultaneously incredibly modern and incredibly ancient. This could equally apply to this house designed by Bawa.

The house is entered from a narrow street into a high walled courtyard. The street elevation is modest and restrained in its detail, revealing little of the interior. The predominant colour of the courtyard walls is yellow ochre, not unlike the colour used in the Cinnamon Hill house. In the evening candles placed in small clay pots greet visitors.

Like Geoffrey Bawa's own house in Bagatelle Road (page 156) the Jayakody residence is a microcosm of the city with courtyards, side lanes, tall light wells, the experience of anticipation, surprise, deflection, framed vistas, compression, spatial explosion, an outdoor terrace, a *loggia*, a gallery, a secretive back stair, places of serenity and peace, a sparkling emerald pool on the roof, baroque

Beyond the entrance gate is a high walled courtyard. In the evening candles are placed in small clay pots to greet visitors.

music, the aroma of Ceylonese food, the sound of a chopping block from the kitchen. One is reminded instantly of Christopher Alexander's 'Pattern Language' and the experience of walking through an urban environment such as Sienna or Jaisalmer. There is the choreography of space and light in complex interrelated patterns, overlapping and coalescing. A myriad moods and memories are condensed into a single house. Overall there is a feeling of immense calm, a sense of timelessness.

Incorporated in the entrance hall of the house are four tall green painted doors with peacock fanlights. The doors came from a great 18th century house as did the huge antique mirror in the hall. Completing the memories incorporated in this space is a magnificent antique timber and glass chandelier. The hallway creates a space of transition between the public and private realms.

The principal rooms are wonderfully naturally ventilated spaces with surprisingly efficient cross breezes moving through the house from the peripheral courtyards. The walls are spartan and unadorned. "This house is not good for pictures," says Rohan Jayakody, "paintings do not look well on the walls". The owners sold their entire collection of Sri Lankan modern and contemporary art for this reason. Only one small Donald Friend painting, displayed on an easel, and 2 works by Australian painters Margaret Olley and Brett Whitely have been retained. The walls are left for the play of patterns of sensual sunlight and shadows of trees, punctuated by a few striking antiques and clay pots.

Elsewhere there are moments of shear exuberance. In the principal bathroom is a large antique stained glass window, casting shards of red and green light across the bath. Another moment of sheer bliss is the view of the tall light well, painted in cobalt blue, that permits sunlight to tumble into the dining room throwing a huge clay wine amphorae, that stands at it's base, into stark silhouette. The grandeur of this gesture is a breathtaking insight into the scale of

Above: The living area glimpsed from the entrance lobby.
Right: Sensual patterns of sunlight and shadow play upon the internal walls of the house. The principal rooms are naturally ventilated.

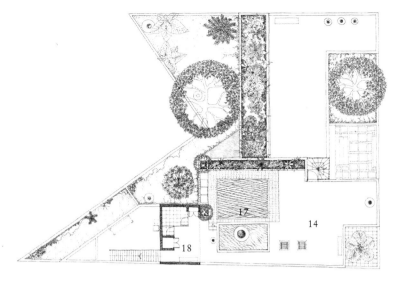

4th Storey

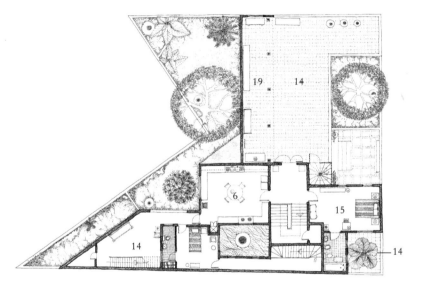

3rd Storey

Above: A huge amphorae is silhouetted against the wall of the lightwell adjacent to the dining area.
Opposite: A tall mature tree casts delicate shadows on the yellow ochre wall of the rear courtyard.
Overleaf: Sunlight tumbles into the interior of the house through a tall lightwell.

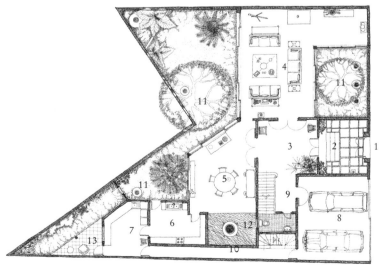

1st Storey

1	street entrance	11	courtyard
2	entrance court	12	lightwell
3	vestibule-entrance	13	kitchen Court
	lobby	14	roof terrace
4	living	15	bedroom
5	dining	16	maid
6	kitchen	17	bathing pool
7	preparation	18	sauna
8	garage	19	loggia
9	stairwell		
10	service access		The 2nd storey plan has been omitted.

Bawa's imagination and his ability to manipulate light and shade and to define space.

The roof terrace is a different world, at tree top level, part of and yet apart from the city. It is accessed from a lower terrace via an external stair enclosed in a steel frame that looks like a enormous bird cage. It is a delightful witty gesture. The lower terrace has a loggia, the roof of which is supported on columns salvaged from a demolished mosque. The rear service stair is intriguing, it might have been inspired by, and provokes memories of, the ramparts of a Medicci *fortezza* in Tuscany or the Stonetown in Zanzibar. These images may not be inappropriate for Sri Lanka has been touched at various times in it's history by the cultures of Arabia, East Africa and was located on the early trade routes from Asia to Europe via the Mediterranean.

In the secluded world that Bawa has created at tree-top level, a small emerald-green tiled swimming pool sparkles in the sun. As if by magic two bright blue kingfishers alight in the lower branches of an adjacent tree. It is a perfectly brilliant house, a transcendental experience. It reflects the diverse cultural in-

The rear service stair evokes memories of the ramparts of a Medicci *fortezza* in Tuscany.

The roof terrace is a different world, a retreat from the noise and dust of the city.

fluences that have touched Sri Lanka.

Many critics misunderstand Geoffrey, say the owners, they assume he designs with limitless budgets only for the very rich, but this is a house of modest proportions. It was built to a strict budget. The site is 18 perches (455.22 square metres). With a built up floor space of 650 square metres the plot ratio is 1.4:1 but if the utility of the roof terraces is added it is probably nearer to a very efficient 1.6:1. The Jayakody's sold many things from their previous home which would not fit into their new house.

The owners speak with near reverence of the relationship they had developed with the architect, "Geoffrey is a genius!" says Rohan Jayakody, while Bawa modestly attributes the house to the owners contribution. On the living room table a stack of books bear witness to the interest of Rohan Jayakody and his wife Dulanjalee in things artistic and antique. He selects a book on the work of the Mexican architect Luis Barragan and reads the following quotation by Francisco Gilardi explaining his relationship to Barragan, which almost exactly mirrors the relationship between Rohan Jayakody and Geoffrey Bawa.

He was a man whose work was well within the sphere of my interests. That is to say most of the people in my circle of acquaintances were familiar with his work. Still, for me, commissioning a design from (him) was like a dream, I never let myself dream. I wonder if you can understand what I am talking about here? The point is that given my age at the time and the money I had it was virtually impossible to think of asking him to build a house for me. It was more unreal than a dream.[2]

[1] Khan. Hasan-Uddin, in The Architecture of Housing (Ed. Robert Powell), Aga Khan Trust for Culture, Geneva, Switzerland, 1990.
[2] Luis Barragan, Noriega Editions, 1992.

In the secluded world at tree-top level, an emerald-green tiled bathing pool sparkles in the sun.

ARYASINHA HOUSE

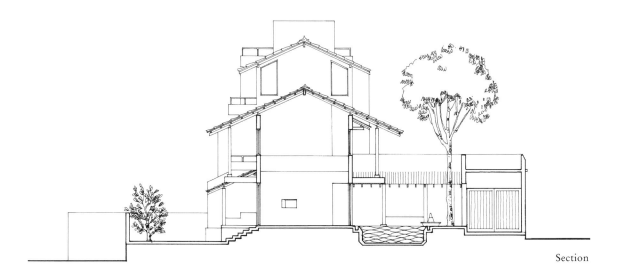

Section

Above: The house is entered from a narrow unmade road.
Overleaf: Cement floors impart an almost monastic austerity to the house. A counterpoint to this is the cobalt blue wall and the cantilevered staircase. At night candles placed in small triangular niches create magical reflections on the surface of the water.

One enters the Aryasinha House from a narrow lane, so narrow indeed that it is impossible for a vehicle to make a right angle turn into the garage. Many ideas are explored here and the influence of Anura Ratnavibhushana's architectural education in Denmark, together with the influence of Geoffrey Bawa and Bawa's erstwhile partner, Ulrik Plesner is evident. Anura's training at the Academy of Art in Copenhagen was, he says, pivotal. As a requirement of the course he travelled to the USA and throughout Europe becoming familiar with the work of Saarinan, Corbusier and Frank Lloyd Wright.

The visual focus of the Aryasinha House is a dark mirror-like pool that occupies the courtyard to the left of the entrance gate. A short corridor, open on both sides, leads alongside this pool to an inner entrance door. A cobalt blue wall acts as the backcloth to the pool.

A cantilevered stair which leads to a roof terrace projects from this wall. These elements are a development of similar architectural language used by the architect in an earlier house designed for his own family at Moratuwa, that was illustrated in *The Tropical Asian House* (Powell 1990). The pool in the Moratuwa House has more immediate impact for the principal circulation routes are around its edge. In the Aryasinha House it is more peripheral to the composition.

The house has a simple plan using a restrained modernist language overlaying an instinctive response to climate. Projecting concrete beams at first storey level support timber columns which in turn provide support for a wide extension of the eaves. This detail provides shade and throws the tropical rainwater clear of the house walls.

The house has rough plastered walls and smooth polished grey cement floors which imparts a monastic austerity to the design. A sharp counterpoint to this is the play of light and shadow on the walls which enlivens the various spaces in this tranquil house. The blue wall in the courtyard has a number of small

The visual focus of the house is a mirror-like pool in a courtyard to the left of the entrance.

The living room opens directly to the pool and stepping stones over the water give access to a roof terrace above the garage.

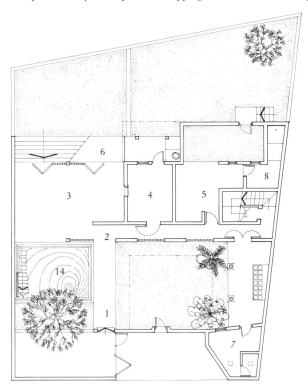

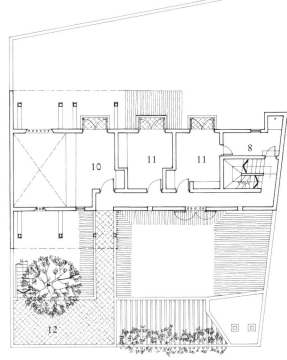

1st Storey

2nd Storey

triangular recesses. In the evening candles are placed in these recesses and they create magical reflections on the surface of the water.

At the very top of the house, there is a secluded roof terrace, accessed by a narrow winding staircase, that gives a view over neighbouring trees to the distant lake surrounding the Parliament House. The built-up floor area of the house is 320 square metres on a site area of 400 square metres giving a plot ratio of 0.80:1.

In a succession of beautiful but restrained designs for houses from the early 1970's onwards Anura demonstrates an ability to produce poetic combinations of light, space and water. The latter is a key element in the Weerawardana House at Dehiwela, a 1972 renovation and alteration for his sister and brother-in-law. His former house at Moratuwa has been widely published and in 1998 he moved to a new house built for his family at Battaramula on the edge of a lake, bordered by marshland. An essential ingredient in each of these house is the limited palette of materials and colours comprising brilliant white and blues on ceilings and walls, and smooth grey floors contrasting with various hues of natural timber.

A narrow staircase ascends to a secluded roof terrace with distant views of the lake surrounding Parliament House.

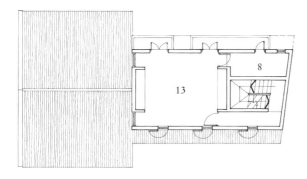

3rd Storey/roof

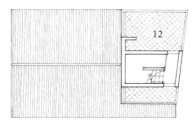

4th Storey/roof

0 1 5 10m

1 entrance
2 entrance verandah
3 living/dining
4 kitchen
5 guest room
6 verandah
7 maid
8 bathroom/wc
9 garage
10 study
11 bedroom
12 roof terrace
13 master bedroom
14 courtyard/pool

CONTRAST HOUSE

The use of a modernist architectural language sets the Contrast House apart from it's neighbours.

The Contrast House is located in a northern suburb of Jakarta. It is within a private gated enclave in this sprawling megalopolis of more than 10 million inhabitants. Constructed on a corner site the exterior of this brilliantly designed 'urban' house is in marked contrast to it's conventional pitched roof 'suburban' neighbours. Part of this urban quality is derived from the relationship of the house to the site. Three-storeys high, it is built right up to the boundary and turns inward to a courtyard space. The house has built up floor space of 400 square metre on a tight site of 375 square metre giving a plot ratio of 1.1:1.

The design is at first less didactic than Sardjono Sani's designs for the No-Body House which employed a Deconstructivist language, but a keen eye will detect an attention to detail and tectonic qualities which characterises both works. There is a studied sophistication in the juxtaposition of materials that is lacking in its more conventional neighbours. Sani has a very close working relationship with the client Marco Kusumawidjaja, also an architect, who was deeply involved with each design decision. There was a close dialogue between them throughout the project and the intensity of this dialogue is reflected in the almost obsessive attention to details.

The house is entered in the south-west corner. The entrance lobby gives access to a vestibule with a spectacular long view of the living area. The living area is raised 600 mm above the vestibule and is accessed via a narrow ramp. One executes a sharp right hand turn around a circular, yellow-painted, concrete column. To the right is the study, a simple glass box with a utilitarian language that signifies 'work' and 'office'. Fluorescent lighting emphasises this contrast with the 'residence'.

Inset in the floor at the base of the ramp is a marker – a rectangular collage of small ceramic tiles, of various colours and patterns. The involuntary response is to glance down to ones feet and then upwards to appreciate the huge volume of the two-storey living space. The contrast in scale is immense. The living room is almost a 'cafe' space, a public arena, in it's scale. The intention is to hang a large purple velvet curtain adjacent to the entrance, a theatrical gesture which will contrast with the simple cement floor.

Thus begins a journey through the house where contrast is constantly exploited. There are a variety of spatial experiences, compressed ceiling heights in one part of the house contrast with the voluminous living space which expands out into the garden. One has the bodily experience of being squeezed into the vertical space accommodating the staircase from second to third storey. It turns at right angles and emerges into a spectacularly natural lighted area. Sani has consciously manipulated spatial experience constricting views, to subsequently offer spectacular long views, compressing spaces then allowing others to leap up in volumetric expression. This utilises a principle of what Sani refers to metaphorically as, "lime and milk".

The contrast goes further exploring not just spatial differences such as narrow-wide, long-short, open-closed, spatial compression-spatial explosion, but auditory and sensory contrasts – yellow-grey (primary-monochrome), rich-ordinary (teak-cement).

The exterior gives little indication of the openness in the planning of the interior.

Above: Beyond the double-height living and dining area is a mezzanine level. There is a contrast in the floor materials: the former is a rich teak finish, the latter a polished cement floor.
Left: The living area and the kitchen open directly into the courtyard.

A collage of ceramic tiles set in the cement floor signifies a change in direction and a contrast in scale.

The house sits on a heavy stone base without visible mortar joints and the initial impression is of a grey monochrome building. Colour is introduced selectively, there are some red terra-cotta painted walls. Dramatically juxtaposed against this are the circular structural columns painted in bright cadmium yellow. In contrast to the grey cement floors is the teak paneled floor of the upper living room which echoes hollowly, when one walks upon it, in auditory contrast to the solid concrete based floor. In the same way the minimalist design of balustrades contrast with the pleasure that one derives from the special balustrade leading to the family room which is designed to give a metallic 'ring' as one ascends like the wind-bells on a temple.

There is a return to modernists beginnings evident in Sani's latest work. In the spatial choreography light and space are major considerations in addition to tectonics. Light penetrates the building beautifully. "God gives us sunlight and it is the only moving element in the composition, so I do consciously use that movement" says Sani.

There are incredibly vivid memories awakened in the Contrast House of Corbusien buildings or of the architecture of Marcel Breuer but remarkably Sardjono Sani says that whilst he has studied Corbusier in great detail, he has never visited any of his buildings. "Architecture," he says, "is a reflective art, it is largely to do with memory, influences come from everywhere, they are stored and reused as appropriate". Sani is now a visiting lecturer/critic at the University of Indonesia's School of Architecture.

The house indicates Sani's architectural progress, for having explored principles of deconstruction in the design of his own house (The Tropical Asian House 1996), he returns here to a more basic modernism – with an idealist client who

The living space viewed from the studio/office. There is a sharp contrast in the spatial quality conveyed by the height, the degree of enclosure and the lighting.

A narrow staircase gives access to the 2nd storey. The balustrade is designed to give a distinct sound like chiming bells.

wishes to explore all facets of living in the tropics. Sani studied at Colorado University where in addition to being influenced by Craig Hodgett and Hsin Ming Fung he recalls the 'extreme' attitude of Douglas Deardon who impressed on Sani that everything should be pushed to the absolute limit. This in part explains the intensity in this house where each element is carefully developed. Each window has been individually considered. The tall fitted cupboard in the family room has integrated steps that give access to the loft space. Sani and the client Marco Kusumawidjaja bring great intensity to the juxtaposition of colours in a limited palette – grey, white, terra-cotta and yellow, and to the detailing of materials – concrete, stone, timber, steel, glass, cement floor and the tectonic possibilities when these materials come together.

Although it is in a suburban area the living room is open to the internal courtyard enclosed by the L-shaped plan, following the basic principles of a house in the tropics. Good cross-ventilation is achieved and air-conditioning is used in the bedrooms only. The courtyard design is minimalist, a single tree sits in a surface of terra-cotta coloured pebbles. There is a remarkable maturity in this latest work by Sani which confirms the promise shown in the No-Body House built for his own family in 1993.

1   entrance
2   vestibule
3   atelier/office
4   living/dining
5   kitchen
6   kitchen prep
7   bath/wc
8   store
9   garage
10 courtyard
11 mezzanine living
12 maid
13 family room
14 terrace
15 bedroom
16 loft space over

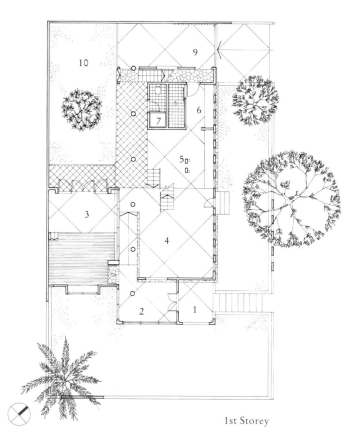

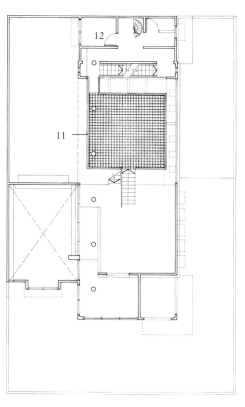

0 1   5   10m

1st Storey

Mezzanine

At 2nd storey level is a family room overlooking the courtyard.

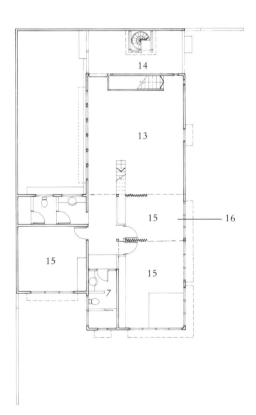

2nd Storey

CARAGUE HOUSE

MANILA, PHILIPPINES 1997

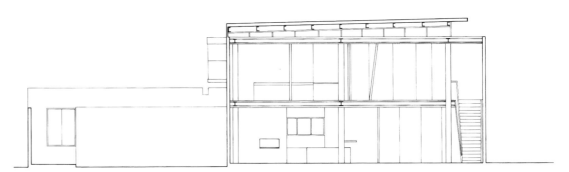

Section

An 'alleyway' behind the high boundary wall terminates in a rectangular courtyard at the house entrance.

I didn't have any preconceived ideas about the house. It took a long time to finish but it gave me the opportunity to look at many possibilities and to solve every condition and detail in a manner which is different to what one ordinarily encounters. **EDUARDO CALMA**

The Carague house is a brilliant modernist solution by the young Philippines architect, Eduardo Calma. Calma is the son of Lor Calma who was one of the foremost modern architects in the Philippines in the pre-martial law era (1960's-70's). The elder Calma is also an acclaimed artist as well as an accomplished furniture and jewellery designer.

Eduardo Calmas' architectural education consisted of five years at the Pratt Institute in New York and Columbia University School of Architecture where a major influence on the faculty was Dean Bernard Tschumi. In between these periods of formal learning Calma worked as a design architect under Carlos Zapata, who was two years his senior at Pratt, and with Peter Pran, at Ellerbe Becket the large New York architectural practice. It was a special collaboration because both Zapata and Pran encouraged open design sessions with all the designers at the start of every project to get as many ideas as possible for form relationships on the table. Familiar forms were discarded and accidental forms developed. Everything started from looking at the conditions of the site. However this process did not question the totality of the work and certainly not the programme. The enclosure was really the only thing to change.

"I see the same thing here in the Philippines," says Calma, "the outside of a house may have a modern expression but the spaces inside remains rooted in an 18th century centralised plan arrangement."

The time he spent doing his Masters was crucial. The avant garde faculty under Tschumi gave him a different perspective in approaching design. The starting point for each project at Columbia was the definition, and in most cases re-definition, of the programme. Instead of looking at architectural history or architectural types there were other models and sources of inspiration from the arts, from physics, from biology and from everyday life occurrences. Calma discusses the interchangeability of signs and recalls, in this context, a church in New York that had been converted to a disco. In the words of Kisho Kurokawa, it evoked "a world of interchangeable signs".

This affected his approach to the design of houses in the Philippines to which he returned in 1992 to become design principal in his father's practice. "Most clients want a modern house," says Calma, "but they already have a certain fixed perception of the use of spaces; a bedroom is a bedroom for sleeping, a dining room is a dining room for formal dining, etc. But the programme can be more open. Programmatic shifts have to be accommodated. In the Carague House, I have designed a second floor that is intended to be convertible, it might be a bedroom, a family room, etc. etc."

"Nevertheless," says Calma, "I work best within restrictions; I dislike a completely open brief. I had one client who wanted to live a secluded existence, not to be seen, and who was also incredibly concerned about security and intrusion, even to the extent of requiring 'secret' exits from rooms and 'escape routes'. At the same time, the client wanted the normal things we associate with a house; daylight, views, etc. The multiple programme imposed on the house was an opportunity to create greater 'richness' in the solution.

There are a number of programmatic impositions within the Carague House designed by Calma for his sister and her husband. The site is part of his brother-in-laws family plot in Parañaque, in the southern suburbs of Manila. It is 15 kilometres from the 'centre' of the city but anything from 30 minutes to 3 hours away depending on traffic conditions (Manila residents never express journey-to-work in terms of distance, it is always in terms of the dimension of time).

In 1995, with the imminent arrival of a young child, the Caragues' required more space than was available in their parents house and this new house was built

The side wall at 2nd storey level peels away from the structure to permit a vertical fissure of light to enter the master bedroom.

1   street entrance
2   alleyway
3   courtyard
4   vestibule
5   dining
6   living
7   kitchen
8   convertible space
9   master bedroom
10 bedroom
11 maid

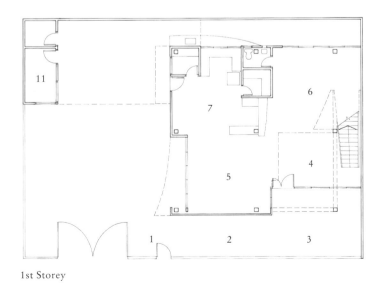

1st Storey

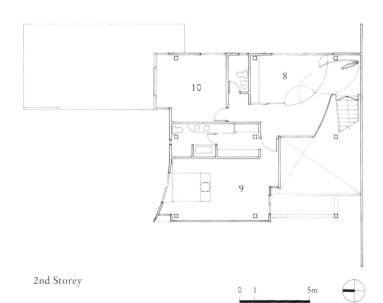

2nd Storey

0   1   5m

Above: Entering the house one encounters a tight vertical space with a thrusting staircase. Opposite: There is an overall impression of space in the minimalist interior: To the left upon entering is the dining area.

in a rectangular plot in their compound which had previously accommodated a guest room and a four-car garage. In the process the garage was reduced to a compact three-car garage. The house was occupied, after several adjustments to the brief, in 1997.

The compound is entered from the street through a large iron door into the automobile court or alternatively, for pedestrians via a simple unadorned, iron gate. A sharp right turn leads to an 'alleyway' parallel to the street and behind a high boundary wall. This narrow 'street' widens slightly to terminate in a rectangular courtyard fronting the house entrance. The courtyard accommodates a small outdoor eating space.

Calma explores the programmatic idea of 'the house as a billboard'. The wall facing the street is clad in opaque marble, the intention being that at night vague images of the interior (private) life can be perceived through the travertine marble from the outside (public) arena.

In truth, this does not happen, for the level of intensity of the internal illumination is not adequate to project any images, though it achieves the architect's intentions not by overt display but by the 'difference' in its form to its neighbours. A blank billboard, if you like, capable of having numerous meanings

A two storey high marble wall dominates the main elevation to the street.

inscribed upon it. Calma intends to use LCP (liquid crystal panels) technology in a future project, so that the opaqueness of glass could adjust to changing external or internal stimuli. LCPs could be used to 'frost' glass when required for privacy whilst being transparent at other times.

The house was also inspired by a clip of Alfred Hitchcock's 'Vertigo' and 'North by Northwest'. "One travels," says Calma, "through a compressed but defined space (the entrance 'street') made by the western main wall and the front wall of the house. One is overpowered (dominated) by the 2-storey high marble wall and suddenly relief from the compression comes in the form of a setback defining the main entrance. One enters by a pivoting steel door to be confronted by a tight vertical space and a thrusting staircase. One might feel invited or threatened. Looking down from the second storey the blasts of light from the overlapping ceilings and slot windows create momentary disorientation. One ends the day contemplating a frozen liquid wall simulated by a heavy grained marble wall that glows from the sunset. It's a surreal experience."

The Carague House is a Miesien box. A double-height space occupies one quadrant on the square plan. The structure is set within the outer skin to avoid underpinning of adjoining properties. Beams are cantilevered to support non-loadbearing outer walls which facilitates a high degree of transparency. Large wall planes contrast with black anodised aluminium framed windows with clear glazing. There is an impression of space in the minimalist interior. The minimalist quality is enhanced by the exquisitely designed table by Calma and works of art by his father. The 12 metre x 12 metre house gives 252 square metres of floor space on a 162 metre plot size which works out at a plot ratio (FAR) of 1.56:1.

The side walls at second storey level, overlooking the garage court, 'peel-away' from the structure to create a vertical fissure of light, the roof slab is tilted and raised to admit light through a glazed clerestory. Internally, cherrywood a timber without excessive grain or knotting is used extensively on floors, stair treads and balustrades giving a smooth texture.

There is a overall feeling of transparency about the house; the openness occurs behind an outer veil – the external high wall creating an intriguing duality. By its form it seeks recognition and individuality (a billboard) and simultaneously behind its external wall seeks anonymity, a reflection of the condition of urban life.

Above: The heavy grained marble wall of the master bedroom diffuses the light of the setting sun and creates a liquid glow.
Opposite: Within the Miesien box there are slight shifts of geometry. Daylight penetrates through a clerestorey window beneath the tilted roof slab.

TJAKRA HOUSE

JAKARTA, INDONESIA 1995

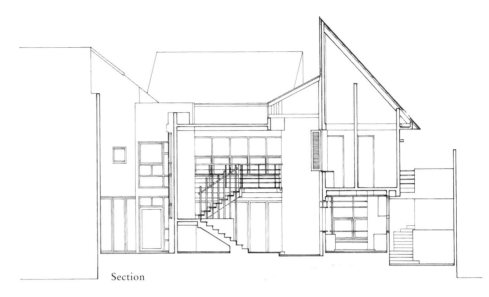

Section

The design of this house was based on the belief that the purpose of architecture is to provide shelter but architecture also has to represent and express the lifestyle of the occupants. Finding clues in the site I was able to optimise the irregular shape.

The house is open to the outdoors allowing cross-ventilation to cool the interior and for daylighting. With the help of a ceiling fan the living spaces are always within the comfort zone.

I was also trying to introduce materials not commonly used in residential architecture. To bring out the character of each material, it is juxtaposed against other materials having contrasting character. **BURHAN TJAKRA**

Above: The architects intention from the outset was that the design must not be constrained by past forms or imagery.

Burhan Tjakra is a graduate of the University of Southern California (USC) and attended Graduate School at the University of California at Los Angeles (UCLA). Professor Murray Milne, the head of Architectural Technology Department at UCLA had a strong influence on him as did Dean Robert Harris at USC. He graduated in 1992 and returned to Indonesia where he worked for three and a half years before he set up his own practice in June 1996.

The Tjakra house was built for his own family; he and his wife have two small children; and it also incorporates his design studio. The irregular shaped site at Pantai Mutiara in Jakarta site has been a significant factor in the form of the house. Tjakra has seen in the irregularity a dynamism which has set up various conflicting geometries and by exploiting these, he has optimised the site.

Thus three rectangular blocks are set up parallel to the internal boundaries of the site. These shapes are juxtaposed against a circular block overlooking the street. These 'positive' geometric forms leave left-over or 'negative' spaces between them. Reflecting the importance of in-between space in the Asian way of thinking, it is these very spaces which become the area of maximum activity and energy. For example the entrance to the house and the principle staircase are located in this space. Sunlight, which amplifies and animates the interior also

1   entrance
2   lobby
3   guest reception
4   office
5   guest bath/wc
6   entertainment
7   pantry
8   living
9   dining
10 bedroom
11 walk in closet
12 bathroom/wc
13 kitchen
14 storage
15 laundry
16 maid bathroom
17 maid
18 courtyard
19 garage
20 forecourt
21 stair landing
22 sitting room
23 terrace
24 child bedroom
25 study area
26 master bedroom

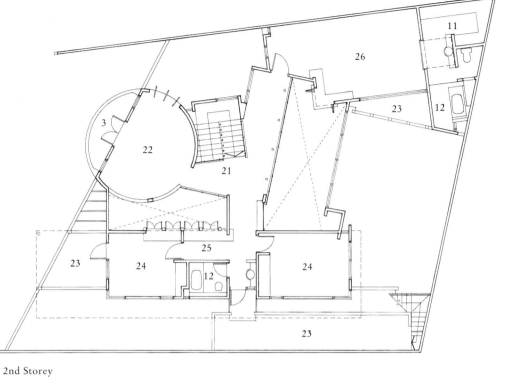

2nd Storey

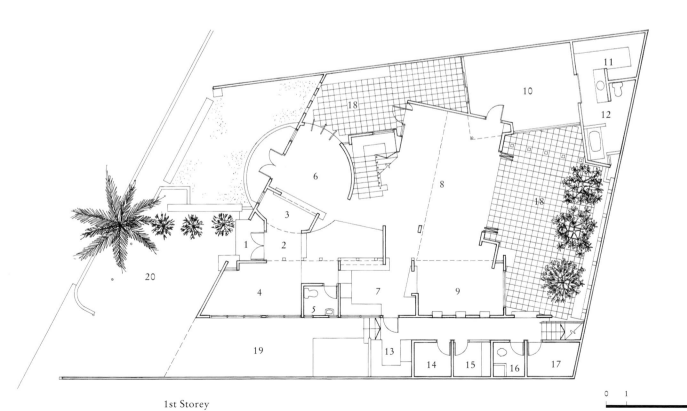

1st Storey

0   1   5m

enters through rooflights in these, so-called, in-between spaces.

The architect's intention from the outset was that the design must not be constrained by past forms or imagery. There is a conscious attempt to introduce materials that are not commonly used in residential architecture, thus corrugated metal sheeting is used for the upper part of external walls, natural anodised aluminium window frames are introduced and unfinished timber is evident in the interior. These are not untypical of materials found in the architecture of LA, Santa Monica and Venice Beech so that some aspects of Tjakra's education in the USA appear to have penetrated his work (Frank Gehry was doing this is the sort of thing in Santa Monica in the 1980's much to the chagrin of his neighbours).

Materials are carefully juxtaposed and their different characteristics define various activities within the house.

Having made such a fundamental break with the manner of designing a town house in Jakarta, Tjakra's house stands out in marked contrast to his neighbours; nevertheless he has not ignored the wisdom of using natural cross-ventilation and two courtyards, peripheral in-between space defined by the principal geometry, promote cross-ventilation.

The larger of the two courtyards is an outdoor extension of the living space. It is pleasantly cool, an urban space, like a small 'public' plaza, enhanced by a koi pool, a tree, a timber 'park' bench. It is generous enough for an evening party or outdoor breakfast, without being too large. The elevations looking into this internal urban space employ a number of 'commercial' finishes. There is a striped canvas awning over the living room door like a street cafe, there is corrugated metal cladding to the upper part of the facade and natural anodised aluminium sliding windows. It could be a pavement cafe in Santa Monica.

The interior of the house is brilliantly animated by the sunlight, which at various times of day penetrates through the glazed roof monitor and strikes the

Above left and above: The house is brilliantly animated by sunlight which at various times of day penetrates through the glazed roof monitor. Opposite: The entrance to the house occupies space 'in-between' the principle geometric forms. Beyond is the living area and a courtyard.

The principle geometry defines ambiguous in-between spaces.

yellow walls of the curved sitting room and creates pure poetry. The complex steelwork beneath the landing, which reminds one of the mezzanine floor of the Atelier Baumann in Vienna by Coop Himmerblau, is another delightful detail.

These devices serve to create ambiguity in the architectural language. The house has an idiosyncratic but witty resolution. The dominant triangular roof form juxtaposes an industrial aesthetic against the domestic scale of the dwelling.

The gross site area is 441 square metres and the gross floor area is 335 square metres giving a plot ratio of 0.76:1.

The urban house in 21st century will be frequently used as a workplace and anticipating this Tjakra has accommodated his design studio within the plan. The entrance lobby serves both office and residence. Appropriately it too is located in the ambiguous in-between space defined by the principal geometry.

The roof light above the two storey high entrance lobby.

The larger of the two courtyard is an outdoor extension of the living room. It is an urban space, like a small piazza.

DIALOGUE HOUSE

Above and opposite: The dramatic roof is supported on a series of inclined circular hollow steel columns.

The central atrium space is like a street, a 'public space' with windows and balconies built onto it: selected pieces and zones of the landscape filter through and penetrate the entire composition. The interstitial, the incidental and non-defined spaces will be constantly redefined by human activities and events within and without.

The fundemental geometry emerges from the rationalised contextualised imperatives: views, light and shade, ventilation, in-between spaces, functional interactions, independence and interdependencies... an ensemble of derivatives. In return the geometry reshapes them.

The realisation of the roofs, low and high and 'free form', is a part of this composition, it reinforces the dialogue between these components... the surrounding landscaped and (future) built environment and the blocks themselves, the public and the private environment... and perhaps there exists subliminal imageries of the energetic open-ended topography of existing dense low-rise, organic urban structures and fabric. The composition of the roof provides not only natural light, shade and through ventilation, but multiple variations of direct, indirect and reflected light with hues and tones at different times of the day (and night) from the internal refraction of the atrium 'stream' and various coloured surfaces.

Mood and time animate and define each other. There is a new or rediscovered awareness of being part of events within this structured environment which project beyond the physical boundary of the house, enhancing the sense and sensuality of the place.

Eventually architecture with a capital 'A' should melt away and the presence of the spaces emerges with the realisation of the human activities (new rituals) and the spirit (new reality) of the space... the new home. **FRANK LING AND PILAR GONZALEZ-HERRAIZ**

The Dialogue House is an extraordinarily daring project for more reasons than one. The house is built within a virtual context, that is to say, it will eventually be flanked by and confronted by other houses within the overall plan for Putrajaya, the projected new Federal capital for Malaysia. But currently it has no immediate neighbours. It stands alone at the side of a golf course and could be termed the 'first' house in the Multimedia Super Corridor (MSC) that will extend the city of Kuala Lumpur in a 50 km long by 15 km wide swathe to the southwest of the existing conurbation. The MSC, a multi-nuclear model of the city, will encompass the new KL International Airport, the Federal Capital and Cyberjaya, a high technology township.

The Architectural Association (AA) trained designers of the house, Frank Ling and Pilar Gonzalez-Herraiz of the Kuala Lumpur based practice Architron Design Consultants had to imagine the future context. They had some 'givens'. The site is a long narrow rectangle with one of the shorter boundaries overlooking an adjoining golf course, with oblique views of a water hazard. The other short boundary overlooks the entrance road and the two long boundaries will eventually be flanked by other dwellings of, as yet, unknown configurations. The developer has stipulated that there are to be no perimeter walls, therefore any privacy that is desired must be achieved by planning and by landscaping. The design was an exploratory process involving a lengthy interrogation of the client over a period of three years. The intention says Ling was, "to put the client in a

neutral frame of mind." In the process the clients may have 'discovered' aspects of themselves which were initially not articulated.

The result is a house with two parallel 'blocks' organised around a central atrium. The name Dialogue, refers to a discourse between these two elements, a conversation that is about the dynamic interaction of forces around the internalised spaces; about formality and informality, about private and public realms of the house, about in and out, about night-time space and day-time space, about 'his' and 'her' spaces, about interpenetration within this apparent polarity, about give and take, and about relationships. The house thus embodies Asian thought processes that see ambiguous in-between areas as being potentially the most dynamic spaces.

The house is internalised, but there are views out where it is known that these will be permanent. "The initial geometry," says the architect, "comes from the site itself. It is a lot more rational than it first appears to be."

The intention was initially to have open grilles at both 'ends' of the house but the clients desire for openness was compromised by their overriding requirement for security and exclusion of dust from adjoining building sites, both in part a consequence of the house being the first to be built. A solution has been reached where there is a combination of grilles and glass. Time is animated and defined by activities outside (golf) and activities inside, and by the path of the sun.

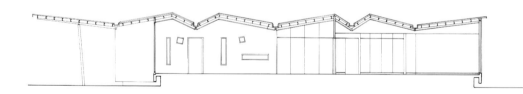

Section

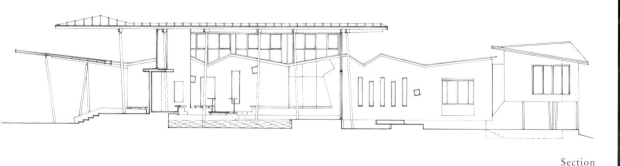

Section

0 1   5m

Above: The roof is a series of tilted angular steel planes which have an uncanny resemblance to the ad-hoc forms of a kampong house.
Overleaf: The house has two parallel blocks organised around a central atrium: a space of dialogue.

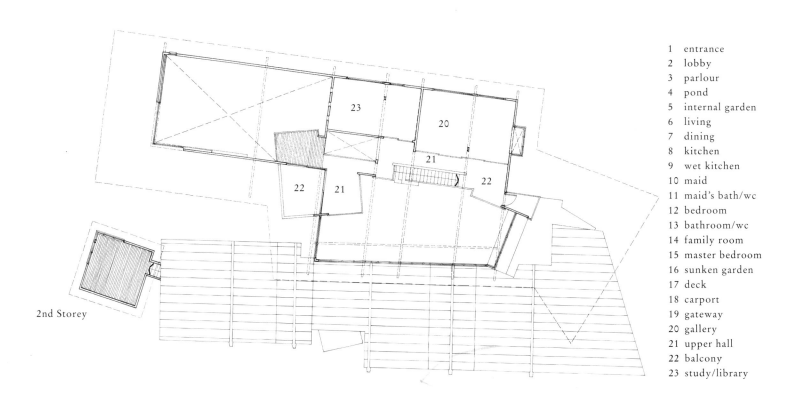

2nd Storey

1 entrance
2 lobby
3 parlour
4 pond
5 internal garden
6 living
7 dining
8 kitchen
9 wet kitchen
10 maid
11 maid's bath/wc
12 bedroom
13 bathroom/wc
14 family room
15 master bedroom
16 sunken garden
17 deck
18 carport
19 gateway
20 gallery
21 upper hall
22 balcony
23 study/library

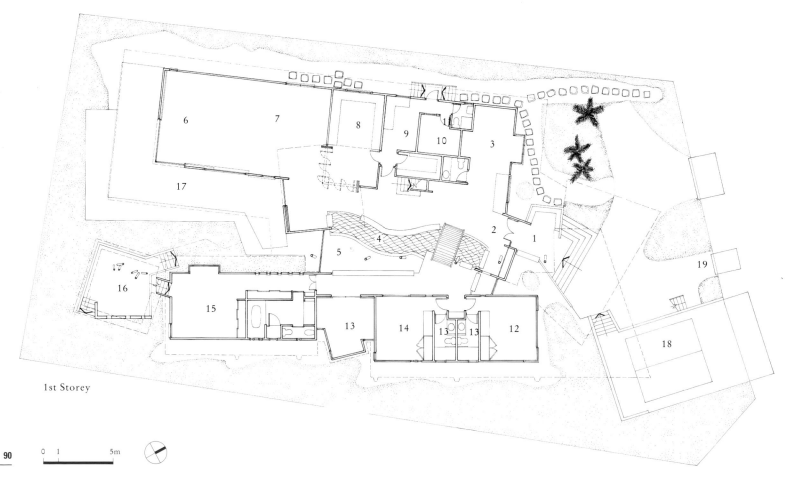

1st Storey

0 1   5m

The architects worked with levels raising the house above the general ground level so that it 'floats'. This raised 'platform' responds to the topography in a manner similar to a traditional Malay house on stilts.

The first view one has of the house at present is from a high ridge to the north west of the site. The most striking feature is its roof form; a series of tilted angular steel planes which have an uncanny resemblance to the ad-hoc roof that one might encounter on an oft-extended Malay *kampong* house. The scale is quite different, but it is sharp reminder of the cultural context of the house and an exceedingly sophisticated though, according to the architects, subliminal, reinterpretation of the indigenous roof. The architects assert that the roof is first and foremost a functional response, not a traditional form though interestingly in Asia the roof is often the most important visual element: it frequently denotes status, as in the houses of the Nias people of Sumatra or the Toraja of Sulawesi.

The roof like the planning is open-ended and invites further 'manipulation'. It is designed with the intention of admitting reflected sunlight. This gives a measure of the passage of time for the mood of the sky invokes responses in human activities.

The steel roof is supported on a series of inclined circular hollow steel columns which 'march' through the house in a seemingly random file analogous with bamboo trees. The architects intention, unfortunately thwarted by financial constraints, was to have the 'steel bamboo' march to the very edge of the golf course, staking, as it were, a territorial claim. The columns contrive to bring an element of the exterior landscape into the interior.

Top and above: There are multiple variations of direct, indirect and reflected light which animate the interior creating different moods and defining activities.

The steel columns which support the higher roof march through the house in a seemingly random file analogous with bamboo trees. These, and the 'stream' contrive to bring an element of the exterior landscape into the interior.

The house is entered via a short flight of steps from the road. The carport is in a semi basement to the side of the entrance. Although there are no boundary walls a gateway helps in demarcating a hierarchical boundary between public and private space. The steps lead to a platform analogous with a *serambi* and thence through the entrance door to the atrium space within. To the right immediately on entering is a 'parlour', a room intended for greeting acquaintances without inviting them to penetrate deeper into the more private areas of the house. The parlour has a direct view of the entrance reinforcing the fact that this is a transitional space.

The central atrium divides the functions of the house. Ranged along the right hand side of the atrium are the kitchen, the dining room and the living room which has a view of the golf course. Facing these rooms and ranged along the left side are guest bedrooms, a television room, the master-bedroom and en-suite bathroom giving access to a music room at the extremity of the dwelling. This room, the wife's domain, is angled to view the water body fortuitously placed by the golf course designer. Beneath this room is a sunken garden which alludes to the shaded space beneath the traditional kampong house on stilts.

Above: Beneath the music room is a sunken garden, a delightful undercroft, which alludes to the space beneath a traditional house on stilts.
Right: Spaces are constantly defined and redefined by activities and events within and without.

Night-time and day-time activities are expressed in the planning with a degree of ambiguity where one stops and the other commences. The ambiguity finds expression in the form of the koi pool which meanders in a linear manner like a 'stream' through the atrium with a bridge linking right and left 'banks'.

The roof over the right hand side of the house is considerably higher than that over the left side. It sails above a two storey space and natural light enters through clerestory glazing from the west. Stairs give access to a second storey above the dining room and kitchen. Here is a gallery that looks into the central space. This visual penetration between the two halves of the house further emphasises the notion of dialogue.

The Dialogue House develops a theme which is common to several houses in this book; that of the importance of the in-between space. The architects intention was to explore the incidental space, the space "in-between", the transitional space. This area of ambiguity which some writers, such as Kisho Kurakawa and Tay Kheng Soon, have pointed to as the essence of Asian thought processes, assumes much greater significance than in western architecture. The preoccupation with this ambiguous space is similarly evident in the Tjakra House and the Corfe Place House.

But the over arching intention is through architecture to explore and rediscover space-time relationships and the ritual responses and events emanating from relationships. Ultimately the intention of the designers is, "to reinvent realities and to discover new realities".

ENCARNACION TAN HOUSE

MANILA, PHILIPPINES • 1997

Section

Above: The house is located in the grounds of a large ancestral residence in Quezon City.

There is something about the Bahay kubo. Bamboo can be 100 years old and it still survives. There is something eternal about this form of house that has survived 800 years. It is spiritual. A Bahay kubo is a shared house. It involves a grass technology and it is a connection with an oral tradition. **ROSARIO 'NING' ENCARNACION TAN**

This house designed by Rosario 'Ning' Encarnacion Tan for herself and her husband embodies a higher purpose than the simple provision of living space. Architect Tan and her husband, who works for a Development Foundation, used the house to explore ways of building in bamboo.

Ning has expressed a yearning to give up practice in the city and to work in the development field, specifically the provision of low-cost housing. For this reason, she felt she could not morally extol the virtues of the *Bahay kubo* and bamboo technology unless she herself lived in such a house and accepted the technology. She presented her ideas to her husband who readily agreed.

The house is located in the grounds of a large house owned by her husbands family in a suburb of Quezon City. The compound has been sub-divided and a utilitarian factory structure occupies part of the site attached to the former ancestral home.

The mansion was originally surrounded by terraces with a swimming pool, a bath house and a tennis court. But the grounds have fallen into decay, the swimming pool has been filled with rubble, the terraces have crumbled and the colonnades have collapsed. Spirits flee from the sunlight to the dark corners of the garden. From the lower level of the garden, the layers of the site's history and it's former grandeur are revealed, a palimpsest of memories is exposed.

On an elevated terrace in the compound, Tan has created a simple square house with a masonry base which is a derivative of the *Bahay Kubo* and the *Bahay na Bato*. The upper part of the house is of bamboo. The floor of the upper

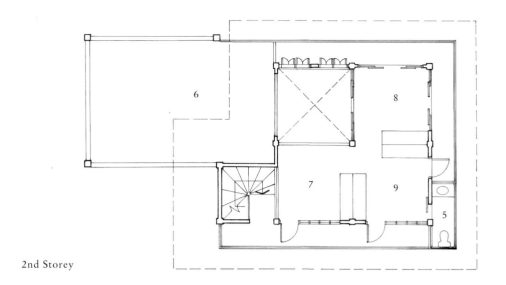

2nd Storey

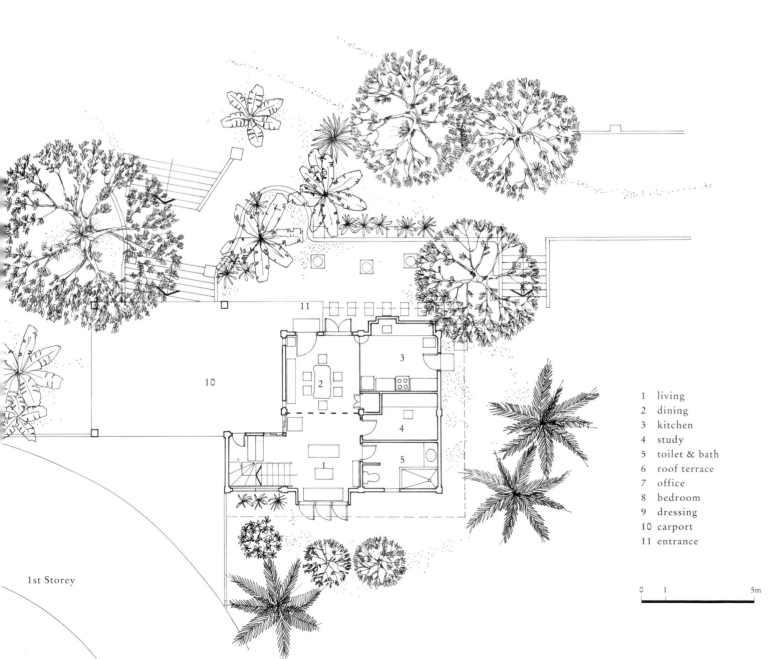

1st Storey

1 living
2 dining
3 kitchen
4 study
5 toilet & bath
6 roof terrace
7 office
8 bedroom
9 dressing
10 carport
11 entrance

0   1   5m

Above: The layers of the site's history and it's former grandeur are revealed in the landscaped grounds which have fallen into decay.

Opposite: The upper floor of the house is constructed in bamboo. The floor is made of split bamboo with gaps to permit underfloor ventilation.

The new house has a masonry base which is a derivative of the *Bahay na Bato*.

storey is made of split bamboo with gaps to permit air flow. Encircling the second storey is an outside corridor; what was termed by the Spanish colonisers, a *volada*, and above this a wide extended corrugated iron roof. It expresses the ambiguous edge and the in-between space that typifies traditional houses in tropical Asia.

Construction of the house commenced in 1992 and was completed, with a small inheritance that her husband received in 1997. The notion of a 'palimpsest' is strongly conveyed by the site, the revealing of levels of family history and memory. Poetically, the top-most layer, the reinterpretation of a *bahay kubo* in bamboo, marking a return to indigenous materials, could be read as rising out of the ruins of a colonial heritage lying crumbled and decaying underfoot.

Opposite: Encircling the 2nd storey is an outside corridor, what the Spanish colonisers referred to as a *volada*.
Above: The upper part of the house is a reinterpretation of the *Bahay Kubo*. It marks a return to indigenous materials and is a significant step in the architects investigation of bamboo technology.

EU HOUSE No. II

THE DETACHED HOUSE
ARCHITECT: **ERNESTO BEDMAR**
• BEDMAR AND SHI PTE LTD
IN ASSOCIATION WITH
B+S+T ARCHITECTS

Above and right: Pedestrians ascend a gentle flight of stone stairs to an elegantly understated front porch.
Opposite: The architect has produced an internally orientated urban house which defies the suburban bias of the regulation governing the so-called 'Good Class Bungalow Areas'.

This is the second house that Ernesto Bedmar, has designed for Geoffrey Eu. The first was the widely acclaimed house in Belmont Road, Singapore, published in *The Tropical Asian House* (1996), which has four pavilions clustered around a black pool and which is located in the garden of Geoffrey Eu's parents house.

This site has a more tightly defined right-angled triangular configuration, with severe problem of overlooking from neighbours and Bedmar has designed a detached urban house. Singapore Building Regulations insist upon 3 metre setbacks from the boundary on the sides of a plot and a 4.5 metre set back on the rear boundary. This is remnant of British building by-laws but it has the effect of perpetuating endless (sub)urban solutions. The designer has with great ingenuity produced an internally orientated solution which defies this suburban bias.

The *parti* for the house is a series of rectangular blocks in a ziggurat formation stepping along the hypotenuse of the triangular site and in the process gradually opening up an open space at the centre of the site. In this central space is a huge existing Angsana tree which has, with some difficulty, been retained by the architect and which is the focus of the courtyard along with a swimming pool. Unlike Eu House No. I, this house does not have the benefit of views into an existing garden or does it have the slightly elevated location enjoyed by the earlier house. The site has adjoining houses just 3 metres from the boundary on two sides of the triangle. Only the third side, at the rear of the site enjoys a degree of privacy.

The elevation to the street is almost entirely blank with a single small rectangular window, a marked contrast to the rather grandiose entrances of neighbouring houses. The entrance to the house is at the narrowest end of the triangular site and there is space only for the vehicular entrance and a pedestrian

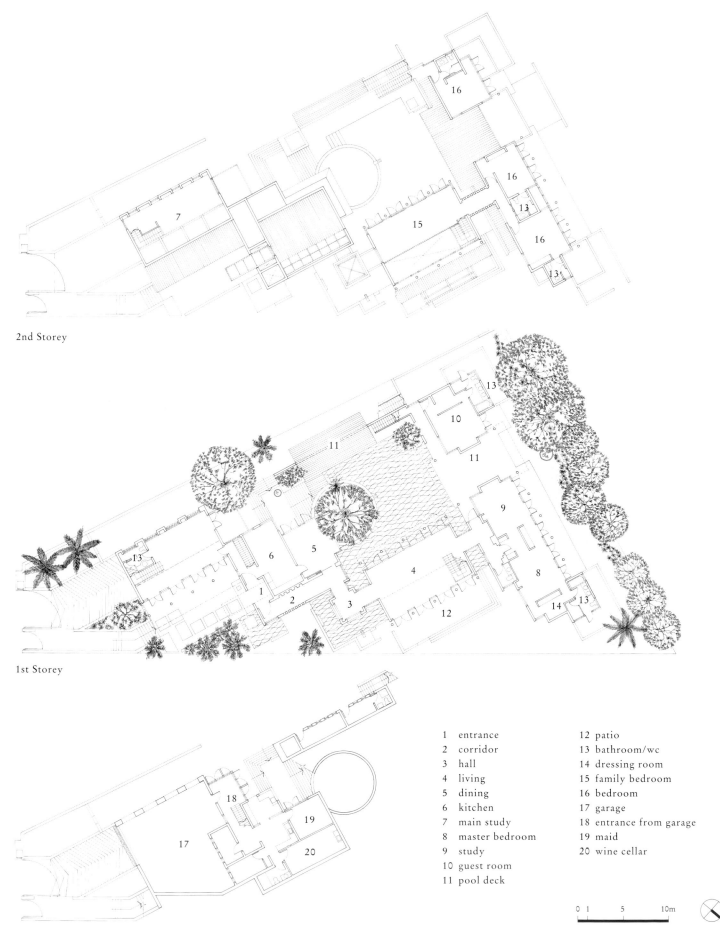

2nd Storey

1st Storey

Basement

1	entrance	12	patio
2	corridor	13	bathroom/wc
3	hall	14	dressing room
4	living	15	family bedroom
5	dining	16	bedroom
6	kitchen	17	garage
7	main study	18	entrance from garage
8	master bedroom	19	maid
9	study	20	wine cellar
10	guest room		
11	pool deck		

0 1   5   10m

gateway. Upon entering cars are driven down a ramp into a semi-basement whilst pedestrians ascend a gentle flight of stone stairs to the elegantly understated entrance porch. The route takes one past the study and family room (which could easily become an office space attached to the residence as work patterns change in the 21st century). There is an alternative route undercover from the basement in the event of inclement weather.

The thought that has gone into the entrance with its granite slabs set in dark grey sea-washed pebbles conveys a quietness and sense of retreat that permeates the whole house. Turning sharply to the right on entering one encounters a stone jar standing in splendid isolation in an external court. It is an orientation point and to the left is a corridor. Early morning, sunlight streams through a screen wall and dances on the floor. Ones attention is drawn to the end of the corridor, to a shimmering blue pool in the middle distance.

Proceeding towards the pool, gratification is delayed. The route choreographed by the architect takes a deviation to the right, and one steps into a small lobby where one is greeted by the sound of water. The source of the sound is not immediately visible. Partially obscured behind a lattice screen wall is a water spout which issues into a pond.

Top: Early morning sunlight streams through a screen wall and dances on the floor.
Above: The architect choreographs a route through the house which gives a variety of spatial and sensuous experiences.

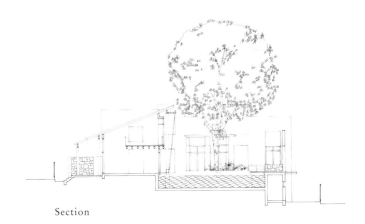

Section

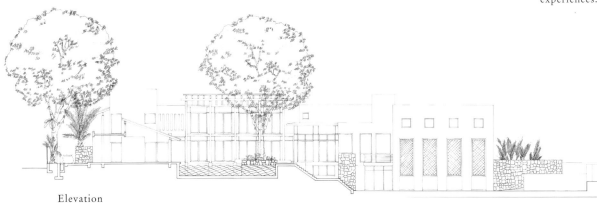

Elevation

Above: A pierced-concrete wall draws a 'veil' across the intrusive windows of a neighbouring house.
Left: The screen wall ensures the privacy of the internal courtyard which is overlooked by the double-height living space.

Above & opposite: 200mm diameter steel columns support the roof and secondary sun-shading devices to the south-west facade of the living room.
Top right: The rear courtyard is a place of remarkable solitude shaded by a screen of mature trees.

A bridge over the pond brings one next into a double height living space with a mezzanine floor above. The spatial quality changes remarkably. The pool is revealed now in its entirety and attention shifts to another space beyond the pool, a timber deck contained by an enormous pierced concrete wall which draws a veil across the intrusive windows of a neighbouring house. To the left of the living area another device is used to ensure privacy. A heavy textile is drawn across the glazed wall, beyond which is a patio which can be used as an extension to the living area should the owner wish to entertain a large group of friends in the evening.

A left turn at the end of the living room brings one to the pool deck and thereafter to the rear courtyard, a place of seclusion and solitude shaded by a screen of existing Kayu Manis, Salam, Oil Palm, Kelay Layu and Leban trees along the rear boundary. The space has the quietness of a Japanese shrine. The house is utterly Asian and simultaneously universal, completely modern, and yet ancient. With its flat and 20 degree mono-pitch roofs this project takes Bedmar beyond the sometimes literal interpretations of the vernacular that one encountered in his earliest houses to an architecture that removes entirely the paradox that Ricouer identified between being modern and yet being rooted in ones culture. Bedmar shows clearly that it is possible to be both.

The primary route through the house continues, along the timber deck, looking back at the transparency of the main living area and then down a series of wide steps to the lower entrance lobby of the house adjacent to the car porch.

Entwined within this primary circulation route are a number of diversions and secondary routes: into the privacy of the bedroom suite, and into the formal dining area. From the pool deck an open staircase leads to a guest bedroom. Activities are overlaid, there are spaces for relaxation, for solitude, for conducting business, for formality and for exuberant play. Indeed the house plan lends itself to use as an extended family dwelling, with enormous flexibility within the layout to accommodate changing family life styles.

I am reminded of the enormous pleasure that I derive from Geoffrey Bawa's House which exhibits a similar variety of moods. Bedmar has come close to achieving, in the Eu House No. II, Bawa's masterly manipulation of space, light and sound.

There are other levels at which to appreciate this house. 200mm diameter steel columns support the roof and secondary sun-shading devices to the south-west facade of the living room. The detailing evokes memories of detailing elsewhere in East Asia. The landscape works with the building, and is neither deferential nor overwhelming. There is an overall simplicity in the detailing. Bedmar has made a major departure in this project from the technology employed in earlier house designed by his practice. Well seasoned timber is becoming harder to acquire and very expensive to maintain. In this house natural anodised aluminium is used. If at first it lacks the warmth and tactile qualities of timber it has its own appeal in terms of the crisp modernist aesthetic and the sense of transparency it conveys.

The site area is 1498 square metres, the site coverage is 517.33 square metres (34.53%) and the built floor space is 928.76 square metres giving a plot ratio 0.62:1.

DORIS HO HOUSE

THE DETACHED HOUSE
ARCHITECT: **CONRAD T ONGLAO**
• **ADR: DESIGN ASSOCIATES**
INCORPORATED

Above: The Doris Ho House is located in Forbes Park, a tree-lined enclave of the megalopolis of Manila.
Opposite: The house is entered through a courtyard with a koi pool and an overhanging pandan tree.

One of the guiding principles that inspired the design was to have the interior living space merge with the exterior garden, allowing a feeling of tranquility and naturalness. Birds fly freely into the house- and the air currents, so important in a tropical setting, keep the interior spaces cool without feeling unprotected from the elements. **CONRAD T ONGLAU**

One enters Doris Magsaysay-Ho's single storey house, from an idyllic tree-lined street in Forbes Park, through a courtyard with a large koi pool and a huge overhanging *pandan* tree. These are remnants and memories of the previous house on the site which were retained by the architect and the landscape consultant Paulo Alcazaren. Turning sharply left upon entering the outer entrance door, one moves around the courtyard skirting the pool, to arrive at the entrance door. This movement pattern is a reminder of the movement pattern in a Chinese courtyard house – never on axis although there is an implied axis.

Thence via a vestibule one turns right and descends two steps to arrive at the core of the house, a high, spacious, square living room with four tall pivoting doors opening to a limestone paved terrace overlooking a swimming pool. The cantilevered roof over this central space is detached from the walls and a glazed clerestorey light encircles the room. The roof sails over the lower roofs which emphasises the height of this principal space. The roof is carried on four symmetrically disposed columns that are visually enlarged to accommodate air-conditioning ducts. Although it has air-conditioning the room has the option of being naturally ventilated.

The main house block has an almost symmetrical plan arrangement. Architect Onglao attributes this to his early experience in practice. After graduation from the University of Santo Tomas in 1978, he worked for some years with an architect-priest who instilled in his young assistants the virtues of symmetry. But viewed in its entirety there is a play between symmetry and asymmetry in the plan which results in a geomantically auspicious swastika configuration.

Upon entering, to the left of the central living space is the owner's private suite, to the right is a raised dining area and an office suite which can also be

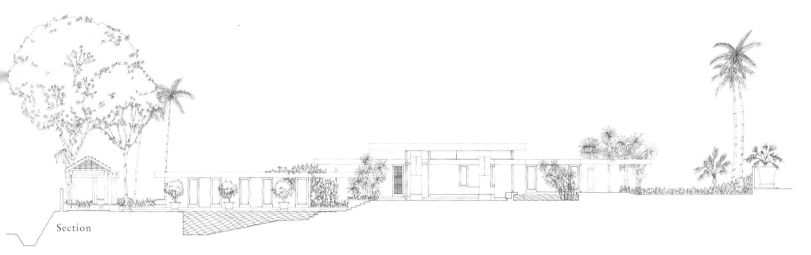

Section

Wide shaded verandahs run parallel to the pool and give sheltered access to the bedrooms and guest suite.

1	driveway	15	AHU
2	main entrance	16	bedroom
3	porch	17	corridor
4	pond	18	terrace
5	living	19	swimming pool
6	dining	20	gazebo
7	foyer	21	covered verandah
8	office	22	study/lounge
9	master bedroom	23	guest room
10	bath/wc	24	service room
11	powder room	25	kitchen
12	den	26	walk-in closet
13	water feature	27	garage
14	storage	28	service area below

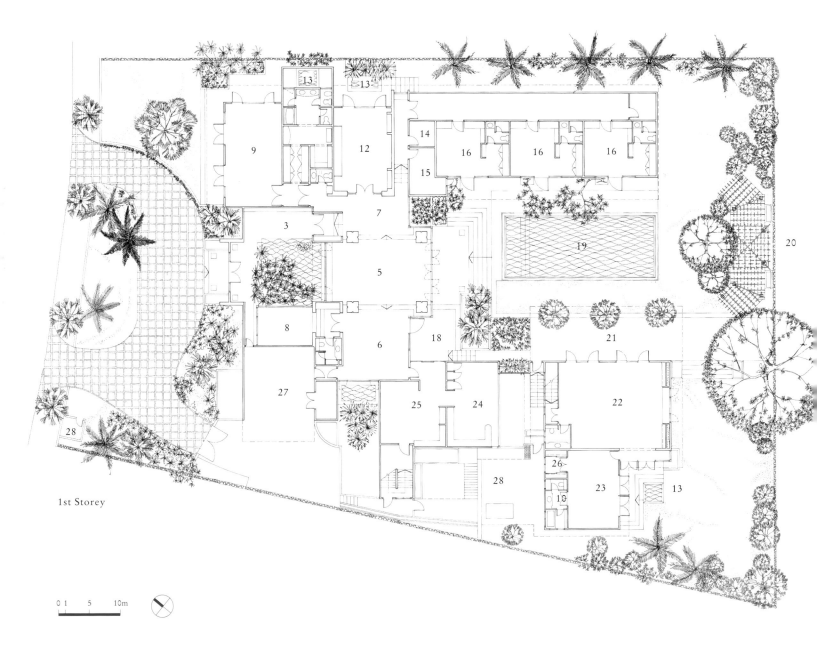

1st Storey

0 1 5   10m

accessed directly from the outer entrance court. The terrace outside the living room is shaded by a five metre wide overhanging roof, a delightful place to take breakfast. Here one senses the 'pulse' of the house. The life of the house revolves around this space at the interface of the interior and exterior. The roof gives wonderful shade and the orientation ensures the sun only penetrates in the early morning. Unless it is a formal occasion, or the weather is inclement, dinner is also served here overlooking the pool.

Extending to the rear of the main block of the house are two wings, one accomodating additional bedrooms and the other designed to accommodate the kitchen and servants quarters in addition to a self-contained guest suite with its own private courtyard. Both wings have a wide, shaded verandah running parallel with the pool. The U-shaped courtyard extends to a grove of huge mature trees and terminates with a gazebo which marks the boundary between Forbes Park and the landscaped Fort Bonificio Development.

The sea green swimming pool with sand coloured tiles, four steps below the terrace is the visual focus of the house. Overhanging the pool are bougainvillea trees. The principal rooms look out to this space. Where rooms are unable to enjoy this view, such as the music room and the master bedroom room suite, they are provided with their own garden courts arranged between the house and the perimeter wall. A number of mature bamboo trees have been carefully retained along the boundary and integrated within these small courtyards.

The house is meticulously detailed using a wide range of indigenous and imported materials. If it has a slightly west-coast-American feel this is not entirely inappropriate for there are strong cultural links between Mexico, California and the Philippines through the shared influence of Spanish colonisation. There are numerous cultural artifacts collected from every part of Asia and America reflecting the owner's multi-cultural heritage. A number of magnificent paintings by the owner's mother Anita Magsaysay-Ho, who has been described as the Philippines foremost woman artist, are displayed in the living room and the music room.

The tall central square living space 'connects' with every other part of the house. Routes are choreographed to the centre and specifically to the dining terrace. It is a romantic house, large without being monumental, which the owner describes as a "peaceful and calm" haven in the chaotic condition of the modern megalopolis.

Above: The daily life of the house revolves around the shaded terrace outside the living room, at the interface of the interior and the exterior.

Above: The living room. A wide range of indigenous and imported materials are integrated into the design. Right: The visual focus of the house is a sea-green swimming pool. At night it is utterly romantic and takes on the ambience of a resort.

WINDSOR PARK HOUSE

SINGAPORE • 1997

The elliptical shaped car port has a roof
suspended on cables from a single column.

The overall idea of the Windsor Park House could be described as discordant harmony'; an aesthetic that is based on the juxtaposition of unfamiliar objects, circumstances and human consciousness. Tang Guan Bee's ideas have intensified the debate on the need for a contemporary architectural vocabulary that is narrative of our lived urban experience. **LOOK BOON GEE**

From the inception of his practice in the 1980's Tang Guan Bee has been acknowledged to be the most avant-garde of Singapore architects. His designs are attention capturing and idiosyncratic, witness recent projects such as Eastpoint Shopping Centre and Bedok Market Place. His work to quote one critic, "exhibits planned incongruities... common to the literary and performance arts which reflect our current lifestyle". These very qualities are exhibited in the Windsor Park House.

Set on a hill, overlooking a suburban housing estate the house occupies a commanding position. It is a situation that the architect has exploited – with a seemingly *ad-hoc* collage of forms scattered across the hilltop, simulating a large art installation. Viewed from afar it stands out from its conventional neighbours with its sail-like roof, transparent walls, and copper-clad pavilions.

Despite its apparently random plan the house is a rational response to the triangular site configuration. The bulk of the accommodation is arranged in a two storey 'tube' parallel to the north western boundary. This is almost the ideal orientation from the point of view of protection from solar insolation. Attached to the south facing side of the tube are the dining and living pavilions, square components, which are hinged and rotated away from the linear form, opening up views to the horizon. The resultant plan has a remarkable resemblance to a MIR space station that has grown by accretion of modules at various times in its orbital course around the earth. Other meanings have been attributed to the house. Tang Guan Bee has described it as an art gallery and entertainment hub for the clients.

After the initial glimpse of the house it disappears from view as the road dips, to reappear, seen now from a different angle, close up and in silhouette. The impression of a cacophony of elements is even stronger. In the foreground is an elliptical shaped car porch its roof suspended on cables from a single column.

The impression of a cacophony of elements is strong. The large amount of glass used for the external walls gives panoramic views out and simultaneously exposes the lifestyle of the household to the scrutiny of their neighbours.

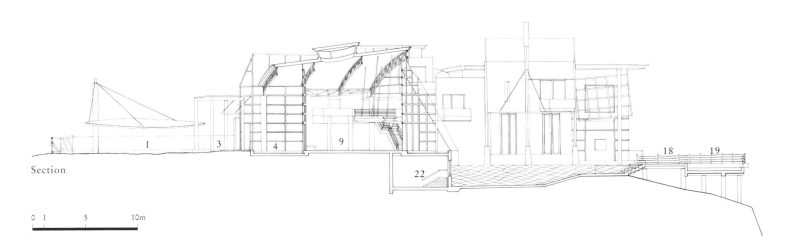

Section

0 1   5   10m

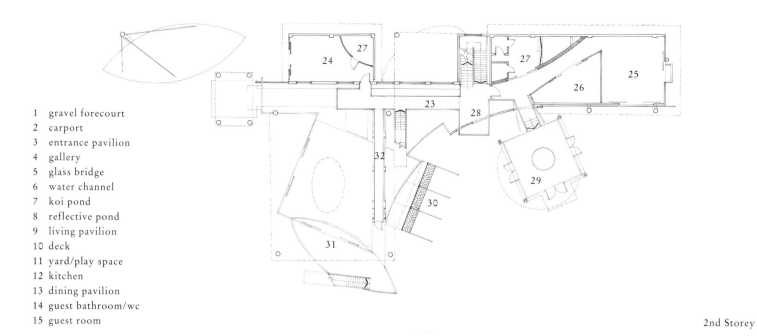

1 gravel forecourt
2 carport
3 entrance pavilion
4 gallery
5 glass bridge
6 water channel
7 koi pond
8 reflective pond
9 living pavilion
10 deck
11 yard/play space
12 kitchen
13 dining pavilion
14 guest bathroom/wc
15 guest room

2nd Storey

16 balcony
17 swimming pool
18 swimming pool deck
19 green deck
20 maid
21 perforated fabric shade
22 video/film preview below
23 bridge
24 study/bedroom
25 master bedroom
26 dressing room
27 bathroom/wc
28 balcony
29 room over dining room
30 aluminium lattice grid
31 viewing deck
32 timber bridge (suspended)

1st Storey

0 1   5   10m

Above: A larger-than-life pivoted entrance
door gives access to the entrance 'runway'.
Right: The linear circulation space is the key
organising device. All accommodation is
attached to this communication corridor.
Overleaf: The house is a seemingly ad-hoc
collage of forms simulating a large art
installation.

Above and top: The imagery is of a orbital space-station that has grown by the accretion of various modules.

Beyond is a huge curved roof over a glazed transparent box that contains the living module. Sandwiched between them is the larger-than-life pivoted entrance door that gives access to an arrival 'runway' complete with 'landing lights'. The imagery of an orbital space capsule that has landed on earth is again conveyed strongly as the visitor walks across the crunching gravel to enter this 'intergalactic docking bay'. The house which from a distance appeared to be integrated into the hillside, in fact sits on a level platform above the surrounding terrain. This emphasises its alienation from the neighbouring houses and demonstrates a recurring sub-theme in this book of the desire to express difference in an increasingly homogenised world. It is a form of escape to another reality. It is difficult to pinpoint exactly the source of the architects inspiration but all these images are not inappropriate given that the owner is in the film industry.

A linear circulation space, referred to earlier as a runway is the key organising device in the plan. Other accommodation is attached to this communications corridor which starts at the entrance pavilion and terminates at the guest bedroom suite. To the north of the corridor are the 'servant' spaces: the maid's room, the kitchen, the yard and the service stair. To the south are the 'served' spaces: the living pavilion surrounded by water, the dining pavilion and the subterranean audio-visual room with its underwater views of the swimming pool.

The notions of viewing and exposure are surfaced by the form of the house. The large amount of glass used for external walls gives the owner a panoramic view of the skyline of the city and of the neighbouring housing estate. Simultaneously the lifestyle of the household is exposed to view from these same neighbours. The living room is designed as a 'stage' surrounded by water upon which the 'performance' of daily life is enacted. It is almost a public space. Suspended above the living platform is a cat-walk which is simultaneously a viewing gallery to the activities below and evocative of a fashion runway for those looking up. One writer has suggested that the sloping glazing is symbolically a big movie screen and that the living platform although public in nature, is surrounded by a body of water which reinforces the idea of detachment and solitude.

This duality is not limited to the living space. In the subterranean audio-visual room the owners and guests can view videos or can, like voyeurs, see the activities of the half-naked swimmers underwater. The swimmers can simultaneously view the activities of those entombed in the video room and revel in their own freedom . And again, in the ceiling of the dining room is a circular glazed void through which diners can be observed from the second storey room overhead. It is not difficult to imagine the cinematic possibilities implicit in all these juxtapositions.

The architect has articulated the transition between spaces to heighten difference. The entrance to the house is through a tall pivoted door which appears to be unsupported. The action of entering the house is thus dramatised as the heavy door smoothly rotates. Likewise to gain access to the living platform, one crosses a glass bridge spanning a body of water just before the space expands vertically into a two-storey living area. Instinctively one glances down, stepping timorously on the transparent surface, before refocussing on the double height space. The difference between materials signals the threshold between activities.

There is a blurring of the boundary between the inside/outside space by the extensive use of clear glass and the almost even quality of daylight which eliminates shade and gives a feeling of being outdoors. It focuses attention on tectonic qualities rather than spatial articulation.

The house is fascinating for it is a reflection of many aspects of our contemporary lived experience in an urban location. Being visible yet anonymous, being in the public arena and yet retaining a private self, expressing difference and yet yearning for solitude, being open and yet detached.

Tang is at the cutting edge in expressing through architecture the various contradictions in life. The conventional notion of the house is inverted, the innermost workings are revealed. The house expresses much of the ambiguity and ambivalence and contradictions in life. The house exhibits none of the whims often associated with an individual house and it eschews the nostalgia associated with pseudo-classical villas. The apparent contradictions and chaos achieve a unity through a strong conceptual framework and an underlying tension that holds together the fragments.

The site area is 2252.20 square metres and the gross floor area is 963.20 square metres giving a plot ratio of 0.42:1.

To gain access to the living pavilion one must cross a glass bridge spanning a body of water.

Above: The house has a panoramic view of the skyline of the city.
Left: Suspended above the living platform is a catwalk which is simultaneously a viewing gallery and a fashion runway.

LEM HOUSE

SINGAPORE 1997

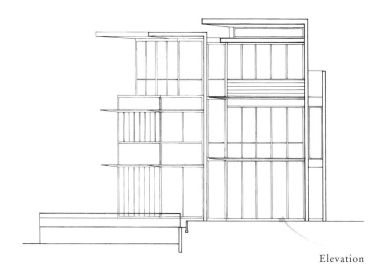

Elevation

The house design resulted from the site: the water of the canal which can be appreciated from three frontages, the changing experience of the water at different levels, and the open landscape beyond. I do not deny that with a full height glass facade there is a trade-off, with some loss of privacy from passers-by along the canal. However as an interior designer, I always emphasise on the feeling of space and this can be achieved through 'borrowed' space. From the outset, the significance of bringing the water and the landscape into every part of the house was an important criteria for the architect. **ALICE LEM**

Having opted to use glass extensively to have uninterrupted views of the water from the house, the next question is how to ground the materials and their expression in the context of tropical domestic architecture. Here we went to great length to detail an entirely operable glass facade. With doors and windows open and the breeze running through the house, one gets the feeling of standing in a pavilion overlooking the water. **MOK WEI WEI**

Above: The solid west wall shields the house from the setting sun and from the neighbouring houses.
Opposite: The north east elevation is designed to give uninterrupted views over the Sungei Bedok.

The site of the Lem House, designed by Mok Wei Wei of William Lim Associates, is unusual in the highly urbanised context of Singapore. The house looks north and east over a tidal drainage canal known as Sungei Bedok and is cooled by diurnal breezes which penetrate from the coast. It is at the end of a cul-de-sac known as Eastwood Way.

The *parti* is a simple orthogonal plan which in order to fit on the site has been split along a 'fracture line'. One part of the plan slides along this fracture to be accommodated on the wider part of the tapering site. This notion of fracture is emphasised in the formal massing. The view from the north suggests multiple fracture lines as vertical wall planes are expressed as projections.

The house plan and section is at one level, a pragmatic response to the real site constraints and regulations imposed by the statutory authority. Statutory requirements stipulate a 2 metre setback along both sides of the house. A 3 metre

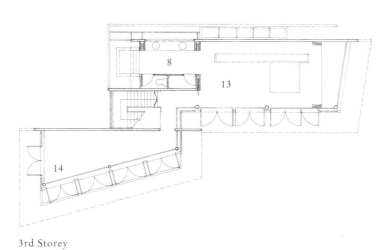

3rd Storey

Above and opposite: The house rejects a
nostalgia for the traditional vernacular and
the language is that of modernism.

1 carport
2 entrance
3 studio
4 kitchen
5 dining
6 yard
7 utility
8 bathroom/wc
9 store
10 living
11 guest room
12 bedroom
13 master bedroom
14 library

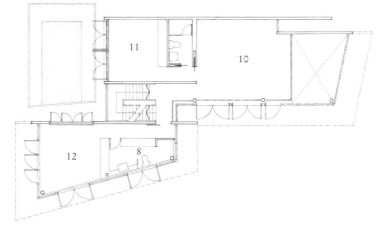

2nd Storey

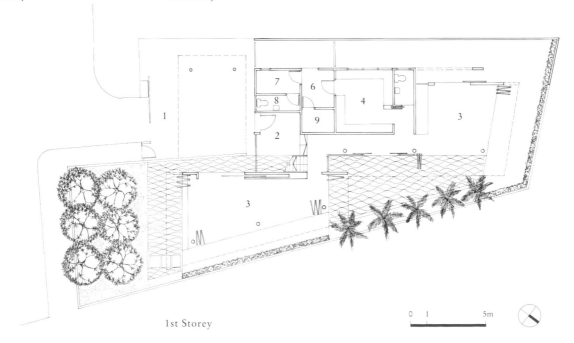

1st Storey

0 1   5m

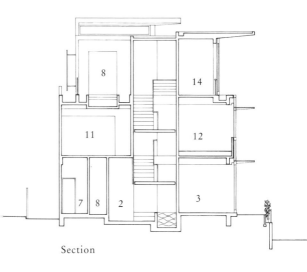

Section

Attention is given to cross ventilation. All the ground floor windows are designed to open.

setback is stipulated for the rear of the plot and a 7.5 metre setback for the front of the plot facing the cul-de-sac. The best views are towards the canal. There are no views of significance in any other direction. Problems arise, for at certain times of the year when the sun moves into the northern hemisphere this advantageous view is unfortunately the worst orientation for exposure to the early morning sun. Given these tough constraints on a site which is just 402 square metres (the site coverage is 38%), the architect has produced a brilliant solution.

Mok Wei Wei has adopted an uncompromising approach and designed the house primarily to take advantage of the unique views. The northeast facing elevation and a considerable proportion of the northwest and southeast facing elevations are entirely glazed with aluminium framed windows and doors. A 2 metre projection to the roof slab enhanced by a 1 metre wide horizontal, perforated-metal sunshading devices at the level of the first and second storey floor slabs is designed to deal with the problem of early morning solar radiation. The architect admits there is nevertheless some heat gain. Solid walls facing west and southwest do however ensure that the house is well shaded from the afternoon and evening sun.

The use of the floor-to-ceiling sliding aluminium window frames and curtain walling results in the house having maximum transparency and enjoying magnificent views in both directions along the banks of the canal and to the northeast over the, currently undeveloped, land on the opposite bank. The reverse is also apparent. Pedestrians and cyclists using the canal-side promenade just ten metres away from the house look directly into the study and the dining room at first storey level which is elevated 1.5 metres above the adjacent ground. Glancing upwards passers by have an oblique view into the living room and the bedrooms at 2nd and 3rd storey levels.

In seeking privacy the three-storey house turns its back on its immediate neighbours. This is not an uncommon response in the suburban landscape of Singapore. A number of contemporary houses express 'difference' and 'individual identity' in this manner. Other examples are the Corfe Place House by KNTA Architects (p.136) and the Khoo House by Ken Lou illustrated in The Tropical Asian House (Powell 1996). But by its very transparency it opens itself to public scrutiny of the occupants and their lifestyle. It reflects a paradox of contemporary urban life where there is often a simultaneous desire forconcealment and exposure: for recognition and anonymity.

One enters the house from the car porch. Running along one side of the entrance lobby is a shallow pond which extends beneath an etched glass window to the garden in front of the study and in the opposite direction alongside the dining room. This 'moat' brings the immediate context into the interior but it simultaneously imposes a conceptual distance between the house and its surroundings and makes the appearance of accessibility an illusion.

The interior of the house is almost entirely white, with white marble floors, white painted walls, large mirrors and etched glass doors in the bathrooms. An open-to-sky roof-top bathroom behind a perforated metal screen is a contemporary interpretation of a Balinese outdoor bathroom.

The house rejects a nostalgia for the traditional vernacular and the architectural language is that of modernism. Flat roofs and planar forms are employed in stark contrast to the transparency of the aluminium framed windows. A pragmatic justification for the latter is that it is increasingly difficult to find good quality timber which has been sufficiently seasoned. In addition, timber needs considerably more maintenance. A large proportion of the windows are sliding-folding doors, French windows or side-hung casements so that the house could function well without air conditioning.

For Mok Wei Wei, the design represents a development beyond the more overtly double-coded deconstructivist language of Tampines North Community Centre illustrated in *Innovative Architecture of Singapore* (1989). In this instance he utilises a more restrained palette and the result is remarkably sophisticated. The client, interior designer Alice Lem, is responsible for the minimalist interiors which contribute to the success of the design. White marble was chosen for its cooling effect and as a backcloth for the appreciation of artwork.

The gross site area is 402.9 square metres, the site coverage is 37.98% and the gross floor area is 371.945 square metres giving a plot ratio of 0.92:1.

Above: The house employs a minimalist aesthetic. The master bedroom viewed from the open-to-sky bathroom.
Below: From the principle rooms there are panoramic views over the water.

BAAN PRABHAWIWAT

Above: Although presently located in a rural area the house 'anticipates' the arrival of an urban context.
Top right: a two storey high car porch is interposed between the principle spaces and the service elements.

The building of the Bangkok to Pattaya elevated highway is stimulating intensive industrial and residential nodal development along it's entire length. By the beginning of the 21st century there could be linear conurbation stretching some 60 kilometres between Thailand's two major coastal cities: not unlike the Tokyo to Osaka corridor. Some Thai families in search of an alternative to the chaotic traffic conditions in the capital see this as a solution, plugged into the highway but with space to breathe.

Continuing the modernist approach that he demonstrated in the Cubic House, illustrated in *The Tropical Asian House* (1996), Vittvat Charoenpong, an instructor in the Faculty of Architecture at Rangsit University has produced Baan Prabhawiwat, a remarkable house for a Dentist, who has a practice in Pattaya, his wife and three small children.

In its present context it is clearly not an urban house but, like the Dialogue House located in the Multimedia Super Corridor south of Kuala Lumpur, Baan Prabhawiwat is a house which 'anticipates' the arrival of an urban context. The lower cost of land also makes it an attractive proposition to live here.

Vittvat has consciously put out of his mind traditional forms, though the house orientated east-west responds well to climate. It is one room deep on plan, permitting cross ventilation. The programme is fairly straightforward without the introduction of complex programmatic issues. The services area and the guest suite are located at the east end of the rectangular plan form and are detached from the main accommodation. A two storey high car porch is interposed between them. The latter protects the house from the morning sun. A curved verandah at the first storey level and a wide overhanging roof similarly protect the west end of the house.

The roof is a shallow parabolic curve formed in insulated profiled-steel with wide overhangs to throw off the rain. It sweeps over all the accommodation like

Cross section

Long section

The architect consciously rejected traditional forms. The roof is a shallow parabolic curve.

The roof sweeps over the house like a huge protective umbrella.

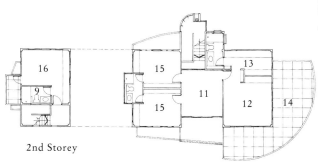

2nd Storey

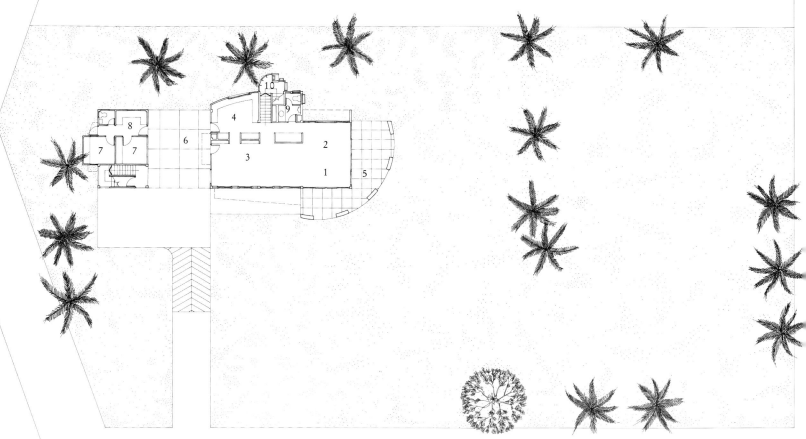

1st Storey

a huge protective umbrella. Details were kept simple for the contractor had not previously used this type of construction. The form of the roof was suggested, according to the architect, by the mountainous topography immediately to the south of the site. Aluminium framed, sliding windows are used because they are the least expensive option. In addition they permit the use of integral sliding mosquito screens.

The house indicates the growing maturity of Vittvat Charoenpong's architecture. It is a well articulated modernist solution with a restrained palette of colours: terra-cotta, sea green and white.

1 entrance
2 living area
3 dining area
4 kitchen
5 verandah
6 car port
7 maid
8 kitchen/laundry
9 bathroom/wc
10 spirit house
11 family room
12 master bedroom
13 dressing room
14 terrace
15 bedroom
16 guest room

0 1   5   10m

Wide eaves throw off rainwater and protect the house from the sun.

CORFE PLACE HOUSE

SINGAPORE 1997

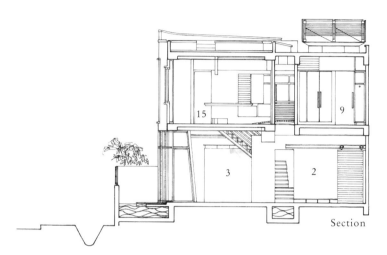

Section

Above: The glazed link between the car port and the house entrance.
Opposite: Entrance elevation. The adjoining semi-detached house, visible to the right, is dwarfed by the new addition which expresses difference rather than deference.

The Corfe Place House raises a number of questions about prevailing values in the suburbs of a rapidly developing tropical city in Asia. It is located in Serangoon Gardens which is one of those private estates, on the outskirts of Singapore, that until the 1990's had changed little. It embodied many of the values of its counterpart in the English suburbs. The semi-detached house type, was probably transported as a housing type to the colonies in Southeast Asia in the early part of the 20th century. One can see examples in Singapore of such housing built for the colonial civil servants and the lower ranks of the commissioned army officers. Thereafter it found favour with developers of private estates for it resulted in cost savings by the reduction of one external wall and the land area needed for development. The image associated with such housing remained remarkably stable until recent years. It had resisted the rapid social and economic changes that had transformed the landscape of Singapore since independence. But rising aspirations of the population, pressure on land and re-zoning at higher plot inevitably reached Corfe Place.

The house designed by KNTA Architects was formerly one half of an identical pair of Semi-D's. After demolition it was rebuilt and transformed to express, not conformity but *difference* and a breaking away from convention. The party wall has become not a 'common' wall but a wall of separation, of demarcation, of defining one's own space. The deference of former times gives way to the assertive expression of one's individual identity.

Difference is expressed not only in the increased height of No. 1 Corfe Place, which incidentally dwarfs its single-storey neighbour, but also in the deliberate choice of a modern aesthetic and materials that are commensurate with this aesthetic. There is greater transparency in the elevations compared with its older neighbour. The roof form contributes to the expression of difference. A metal clad pod containing the mechanical services equipment and water tanks

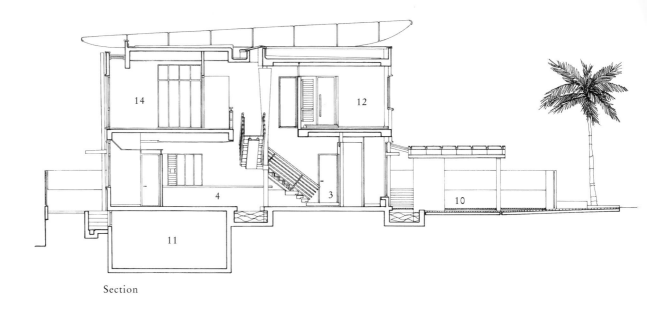

Section

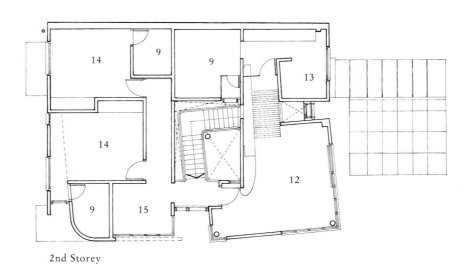

2nd Storey

1 entrance
2 lobby
3 living
4 dining
5 kitchen
6 outdoor kitchen
7 guest room
8 utility
9 bath/wc
10 car port
11 basement/music room
12 master bedroom
13 dressing room
14 bedroom
15 family/study room

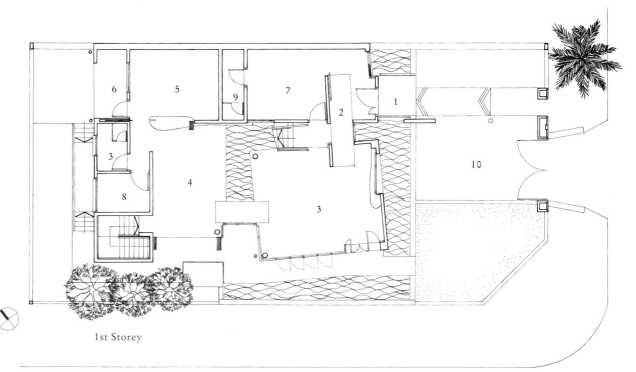

0   1   5m

1st Storey

The entrance court and the car port.

Above: The inverted conical top of the central column.

Opposite: The central column is the pivot of the living space. On the left is a bridge to the dining space.

projects above the flat concrete roof. There is provision too for solar panels for hot water heating.

The plan further emphasises difference by the manner in which geometry is manipulated in the newer house. A sharp incision has been made in the front elevation and a second incision in the side elevation. With the delicate skills of a surgeon the architect has cleaved the living space from the rest of the dwelling, which is aligned with the party wall, and twisted it. A fissure has been created in the plan, a crevasse, through which light streams down from a glazed aperture in the roof. The narrowness of the site limits this fractional shift of geometry to just 5.5 degrees.

The displacement of the living 'platform' is further emphasised by its' isolation within a shallow pond. The principal vertical circulation element is located within the fissure, a steel staircase, which is hinged around a vertical steel column and which negotiates a route through the pressing sides of the crevasse to the upper level. Four bridges, like stretched tendons provide the link between the functional elements and exploit tightly compressed vistas from within the crack.

The almost *even* quality of light in the interior resulting from the transparency and the light from above focuses attention on tectonics. Unlike Geoffrey Bawa's houses which are about the manipulation of light and shade with immense contrast, the Corfe Place House fascinates by the shifting of geometry and the resolution of joints between materials.

The main living space opens out to the perimeter garden. But nature is not welcomed within, there is a clear distinction between the constructed and the natural world. The sliding doors can be opened to allow breezes to enter, but this house is not primarily concerned with climatic response. There is another agenda. The house is an internalised experience. Water is the only connection, it flows from inside to outside, and it defines activity areas on plan.

The house is an exquisite object. Like the widely published Check House completed by the practice in 1994, it is remarkable for the precision of the details, the delicate almost fastidious, attention to tectonics. One detail, the welding of the steel staircase, falls short of these high standards and it is all the more jarring for that. Notwithstanding this comment KNTA have produced a minimalist statement with a limited palette of materials.

The site area is 291.40 square metres and the gross floor area is 306.68 square metres giving a plot ratio of 1.052:1. In the Asian metropolis of the 21st century the ability to create such drama in a tight suburban setting will be invaluable.

BAAN IMPUNTUNG

BANGKOK, THAILAND 1977-1997

Elevation

Above: Water is an important element in the design. There is a shallow pool alongside the house entrance.
Opposite: The external stair has a balustrade in the form of a naga, a water symbol which in Sanskrit means serpent.

Vira Impuntung is an Associate Professor in the School of Architecture at Silpakorn University in Bangkok. Vira graduated from the same University in 1975 and two years later designed an inexpensive minimalist modern house in the long-established district of Bangkok Yai. This is the old city of Bangkok. The house is less than thirty minutes from the University using a combination of transportation modes. Walking from the Silpakorn Campus, which is in the heart of the old city, adjacent to the Royal Palace, Vira boards a ferry to cross the Chao Phraya River and from the landing jetty on the opposite bank, the familiar *tut-tuts* ply the route to the end of the narrow lane that leads to his house. The lane, thronged with street hawker stalls, weaves its way past the local fresh food market and fish market.

Acquaintances describe Vira as a humble man who lives in a simple unpretentious manner. This is evident in the manner he uses his house and which fashions the spaces. Vira sits cross legged on the floor, at a low table, when using his computer much as one would do in an indigenous Thai house. Similarly, when reading, he sits at another low table alongside a shallow fish pond in the study area.

Describing a traditional Thai House in the book *Tropical Asian Style* (Tettoni 1997), Warren writes that, "traditionally, Thais ate, slept and enjoyed social life on the floors of their houses. Furniture tended to be of only the most basic type: a four storage containers made of bamboo, often lacquered for better protection, woven reed mats, some cushions to lounge against, and perhaps a cabinet to hold foodstuffs and a low table or two."

Water is an important element in the design of the house. There are several ponds incorporated within the house and surrounding garden with a wide variety of fish and they have a calming influence upon the house. Perhaps, to quote Sumet Jumsai in the epilogue to the book *Naga: Cultural Origins in Siam and*

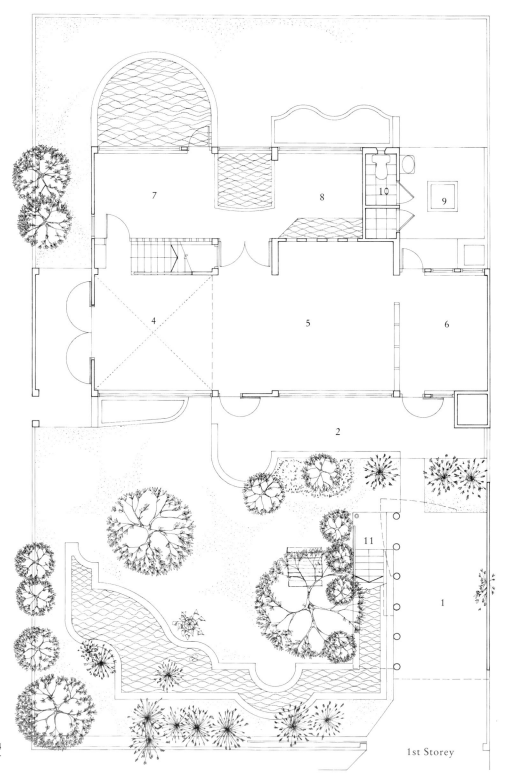

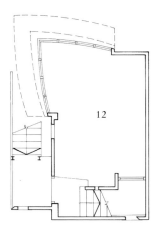

1st Storey

2nd Storey

The house is furnished in a minimalist manner. A computer sits upon a low table which the owner uses sitting cross-legged upon the floor.

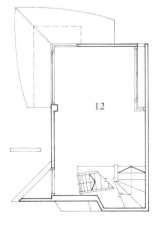

3rd Storey

4th Storey

1 carport
2 verandah/terrace
3 entrance
4 living
5 dining/pool table
6 kitchen
7 study/computor
8 reading
9 yard
10 bath/wc
11 stair to studio
12 studio
13 meditation area

0   1   5m

The three storey extension to the 1970's house clings like an epiphyte to the gable of an adjoining terrace house.

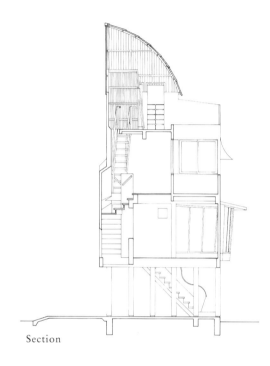

Section

An external stair gives access to the second storey.

the West Pacific, "aquatic influences still exist and, though dormant for much of the time, resurface.... unexpectedly."

The sparse furnishings in the house add to the ambiguity in the use of space. One glaring anachronism is evident: a pool table sits beneath an overhead light. It is a curious juxtaposition against the quiet introspective qualities of the house.

The 1977 house has served Vira and his wife well for 20 years, but in 1997 they added a new four-storey annex incorporating a two storey studio above the car porch and with a roof terrace and meditation area. The new extension is at right angles to the original house and it is built against the gable end of an adjoining row of terrace houses, in the process becoming semi-attached. The narrow vertical form is in sharp contrast to the existing house and encapsulates the dilemma of contemporary city living where, with land in short supply, the only way to acquire more floor space on a limited site area, is to build vertically. The new extension clings like an epiphyte to the adjoining gable: in effect attaching itself to the structure and yet declaring, by its language that it is different. The old house and new annex embrace a garden incorporating informal planting and fish ponds.

The 1997 extension and the old house are both designed without excessive ornamentation, indeed both are minimalist compositions. The new extension is raised on *pilotii*, in the manner of traditional houses in Bangkok. It leaves a space beneath which is used as a car porch and entrance lobby. The upper floors might conceivably form a real refuge from flood water to which Bangkok succumbs every year.

Access to the second storey is via an external staircase which is another feature of traditional dwellings. The balustrade of this stair is in the form of a *Naga*, a water symbol which in Sanskrit means serpent. The second and third storeys are used as a design studio and at roof level is an open-to-sky platform, used for meditation, alongside yet another small fish pond. It overlooks the roofs of adjoining low-rise timber houses with their asbestos roofs. This tiny roof-top space has a sense of isolation which is increased by the act of climbing an almost vertical steel staircase to gain access.

An almost vertical stair gives access to the meditation platform at roof level.

LIM HOUSE

KUALA LUMPUR, MALAYSIA 1976-1997

Elevation

Above: The original (now the secondary) entrance to the house.
Opposite: Upon entering the house one encounters a four storey high atrium space. The structure makes extensive use of recycled timber.
Overleaf: Looking across the atrium the permeable nature of the house is apparent. The space is naturally ventilated.

In 1976, Jimmy Lim acquired an ordinary two-storey detached dwelling which sits upon high ground in a residential suburb of the Malaysian capital of Kuala Lumpur. For two decades he has used the house as the research centre for ideas about building in the tropics, constantly extending and adding to the structure. The old house becomes a body on which subsequent accretions cling like epiphytes. There are a variety of balconies, verandahs, shading, filtering and ventilation devices, lattice screens, louvres, sails, blinds, wind stacks and other details intended to cool the house and to induce air-movement. It is in every sense a tropical house with air-conditioning used only in the bedrooms and music room.

It is also a test-bed for materials and for timber detailing. Many of the robust timber jointing details developed here were later used in the Precima House and the Eu House (now known as the Tang House) which were published in *The Asian House* (1993) and the Salinger House published in *The Tropical Asian House* (1996). Lim's chosen materials are timber and over-burnt brick for load-bearing purposes which are left exposed and unplastered. Asked to justify the use of tropical hardwoods in his houses, Lim will answer with conviction that this is far more ecologically sound than the use of timber as formwork for poured concrete construction . He will point to the fact that CO_2 remains fixed in timber that is unprocessed. He can also point to the extensive use of recycled timber beams, post and lintels from demolished buildings throughout the house.

Within the house Lim has orchestrated a variety of spatial experiences and created an atmosphere of stage-sets not unlike a Shakespearean theatre with fly-tower, front stage, backstage and a sense of impermanence and change. There are places from which to view the activity in the house and to be observed. This sense of the theatrical is heightened by the presence of unclothed female tailors dummies which occupy vantage points in the upper galleries, inhabiting the

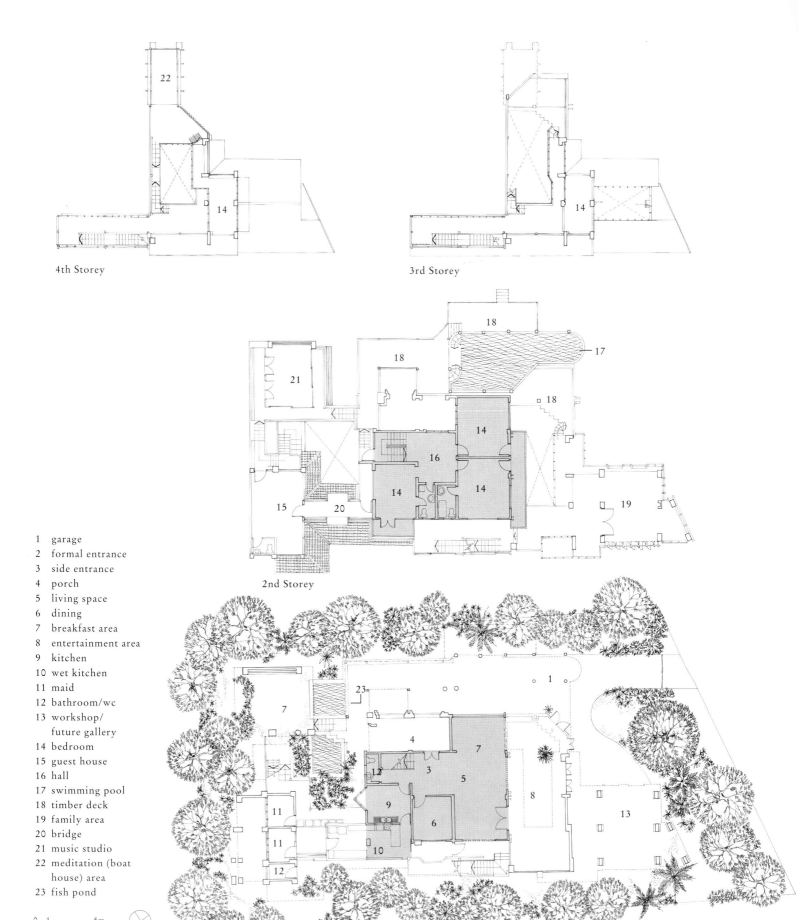

1 garage
2 formal entrance
3 side entrance
4 porch
5 living space
6 dining
7 breakfast area
8 entertainment area
9 kitchen
10 wet kitchen
11 maid
12 bathroom/wc
13 workshop/
    future gallery
14 bedroom
15 guest house
16 hall
17 swimming pool
18 timber deck
19 family area
20 bridge
21 music studio
22 meditation (boat
    house) area
23 fish pond

4th Storey

3rd Storey

2nd Storey

1st Storey

0 1   5m

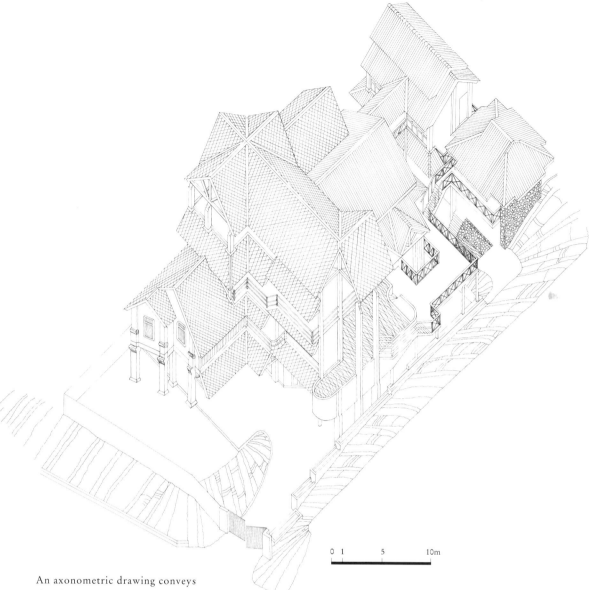

0 1   5   10m

An axonometric drawing conveys the ad-hoc nature of additions and alterations over time. For clarity trees have not been indicated. Further changes have been made since this drawing was completed.

space and in the process, conveying the anonymity of urban life where one might dress (or undress) in a risqué fashion and yet not be censured.

The house is analogous with a city in constant change and evolution. It is simultaneously a research centre, a resort, a residence, a workplace, a museum, a music academy, a resource library, a meditation centre, an antique shop, a garage, a restoration yard, an aviary, an observatory, an ancestral home and a temple.

There are a variety of moods in the house: quiet restful nooks and corners, formal and informal places, expansive semi-public places, a soaring atrium and precarious vertigo-inducing bridges over which one might imagine that Fagin of "The Fiddler on the Roof" might appear .

The spaces that Lim creates are quite unlike the more 'solid' space bounded by walls that one experiences in the architecture of Geoffrey Bawa. Lim's spaces are light and ephemeral, walls dissolve and are ambiguous. Sunlight is filtered by rattan 'chick blinds', timber screens, and by the recurring feature of Lims' work, a 'ridge-light' allowing soft diffused sunlight to wash the spaces below. There is an absence of the modernist delineation of functional use of space. It is difficult to put names to them, for spaces constantly change their function, each succes-

The link from the swimming pool deck to the music studio.

The permeable walls of the house become apparent when one enters the compound.

Above: Bridges and walkways link the various 'living platforms'. The house has grown by accretion.
Opposite and below: The latest addition is a meditation space at 4th storey level (also known as the boat area). A number of opening devices on the roof act as 'sails' to catch the wind and assist in cooling the interior.

sive extension of the house causes an adjustment of living patterns. On every occasion one visits the house the breakfast room has moved! Each new growth node gives the house new life, whilst other areas 'decay' and await 'remedial surgery' which brings with it renewal and rehabilitation for other uses. There is simultaneously a structure and order within the resultant chaos.

The house is akin to a chameleon, it constantly changes its mood and 'colour'. It affirms the Asian notion of in-between and ambiguous spaces as being areas of maximum energy and vitality. It can also be read as a palimpsest with layers of memory being evoked and where new meanings are constantly being inscribed and re-inscribed upon the text. Locked into the house are traces of the life, passions and loves of the owners. There are diverse cultural references from Malaya, China and Australia, where Lim studied architecture: silk flowers, Chinese 'good-luck signs, dark antique Chinese furniture, *kopi tiam* chairs and tables, vintage cars in various stages of maintenance and restoration, old safes, books, ceramics copper pots, and red lanterns. Classical music drifts from the grand piano in the glass-enclosed music room, to merge with CNN Live at breakfast. Several Great Dane dogs, the height of a man when they stand on their hind quarters, prowl the house.

The house is the architectural equivalent of a cult book of the 1960's, which could be entitled 'The Zen Guide to House Building'. It obeys the maxim , "If it ain't broken, don't fix it."

In Asian cities there is a high rate of obsolescence created by consumer markets and there is constant wastage of resources caused by the rezoning of cities at higher plot ratios with the consequent demolition of quite serviceable structures. The Lim House illustrates the robustness of a structure that has grown in a sustainable manner, without recourse to demolition and rebuilding. It has valuable lessons to teach about resource conservation, recycling, continuity and change.

BAWA HOUSE

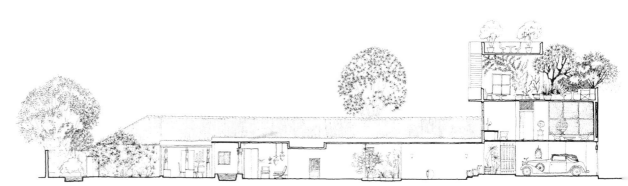

Section

Upon entering the house one proceeds along a corridor which terminates with a tiny courtyard bathed in sunlight.

Geoffrey Bawa's house in Bagatelle Road, Colombo is the amalgamation, reconstruction and adaptation, over several years, of four smaller urban houses in Bagatelle Road. The result is a complex labyrinth of corridors and rooms that nevertheless has a distinct underlying order and legibility. It is as though a city has been condensed into a single dwelling.

Metaphorically the corridors are streets and the open-to-sky courtyards and light wells are plazas. One experiences compression and expansion, deflection and anticipation, light and shade, silent places, fountains and trees. Bawa choreographs these urban elements to create a constantly changing spatial experience as one moves through the house.

The primary route commences at the entrance. In the middle distance, at the end of a long white corridor is a sunlit space. Arriving here, one is brought to a momentary halt: a small fountain trickles into a pool and a tree forces its way skywards, twisting and tortured, its roots like tentacles clinging to the walls for stability. To the left is a *trompe l'oeil* of a pastoral scene by Donald Friend.

These details are absorbed, before the corridor shifts direction sharply to the right. Framed in a doorway is a verandah which is the symbolic centre of the house within hailing distance of the kitchen, a short walk to the dining room and a few steps away from the master bedroom.

The verandah opens onto a courtyard with the morning sun glinting on a small square pool. The shimmering image is reflected onto the soffit of the room. To the left of the door is another painting by Donald Friend. In an adjoining white courtyard, bathed in light is a small sculpture also by Friend for whom Geoffrey designed houses in Bali in the 1970's.

In the dining room, the chair at the head of the long dining table, is a vantage point from which to view a framed vista terminating with the same Donald Friend sculpture. From this same vantage point is another view out to a cobbled

Alongside a shallow pool is a *trompe l'oeil* by Donald Friend. A tree forces its way skyward.

Above: A small fountain gently
trickles into the pool. Sunlight glints
on pebbles beneath the rippled surface.

courtyard with a gnarled old tree and the patina of age ingrained on the walls.

The house is both a residence and Bawa's work place. To the right of the entrance is the office. The second-storey is a large reception room over the office and above this is the roof garden. These areas of the house were acquiring a slight air of neglect since Geoffrey could not climb up there easily but to remedy this in 1997 an elevator was installed. The view from the roof is spectacular, of adjoining house roofs with wonderful trees in blossom growing from internal courtyards. This is an aspect of urban houses often neglected for when all at ground level is polluted, congested and life threatening, there is a great relief in emerging at a roof garden, with the perfume of flowers and stolen vistas.

Building Regulations unwittingly force certain solutions. In cities such as Singapore the idea of setbacks along the side of the house forces a constant re-emphasis of 'suburbia' with isolated bungalows. In Sri Lanka, the building codes permit a maximum footprint of 66%. It produces very dense morphologies. Houses are often built up to the boundary with internal courts giving privacy and protection.

The pleasure of the Bawa house comes in the framing of internalised vistas. The choreography is almost like a dance or theatre, of sensual experiences of point and counterpoint, of light and shade, of openings and closure, of compression and unfolding, of 'hereness' and 'thereness' (to use Gordan Cullen's 'Townscape' terminology).

The house is revealed as a 'city' of myriad moods and experiences, of dark corners, of principle routes, of solitude, of gaiety, of exposure, of seclusion, of privacy and of public display. A city of visual and tactile details: a handrail, a painting, a bronze object, a door, a reflection, a derelict byway, roots of a tree, diffused light through a glass door and a drop in a pool. And a city of contrasting materials: wood parquet, cement, cobblestones and bricks. The house expresses at every turn the cycle of life with inevitable decay... and rebirth.

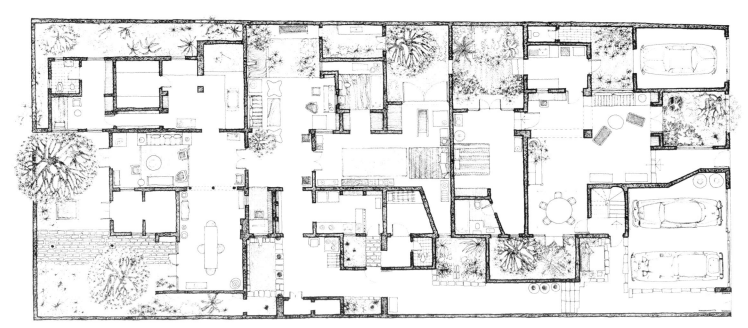

1st Storey

Above: One of several courtyards which permit light to penetrate into the house and which give constantly changing spatial experiences.
Below: From a vantage point in the dining room is a view to a cobbled yard with the patina of age, ingrained on the walls.

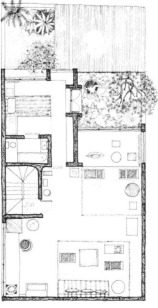

2nd Storey

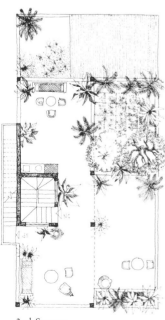

3rd Storey

Above and opposite: The pleasure of the house comes from the framing of internalised vistas with a myriad moods.

TESORO HOUSE

Above: The entrance to the Tesoro residence, a simple square ancestral house built in the 1930's.
Right: The verandah of the house overlooks a courtyard and the entrance to the Patis Tesoro boutique housed in an annex.

The Tesoro House in San Juan, Manila was built in the 1930's and acquired by Patis Tesoro and her lawyer husband in 1975. The renovation and interior decoration of the house was conceptualised by Patis Tesoro who is the Philippines most highly acclaimed fabric and wedding gown designers as well as a tireless activist for the rights of working women and the protection/conservation of traditional materials and skills. Her house in San Juan was originally a simple square ancestral house but it has become progressively an atelier, a boutique (by appointment only), showroom, staff dormitory, office and headquarters to The Katutubing Filipino Foundation. This pattern of multiple use is common in Manila and in other Asian cities not touched by the western concept of functional zoning of cities.

Several dozen women are employed in the Tesoro cutting and sewing operations in the atelier at the rear of the house while her front office, fitting rooms and fabric display is in an annex to the original house. Patis Tesoro continually trains apprentices within the premises in sketching, hand-painting, beading, embroidery and even pattern-making. She also instructs them in the use of colour combination, proportions in drawing and painting and composing intricate embroidery and beading patterns.

Outwardly, the house looks no different to any other house in Wilson Street. A robust iron gate and high walls protect the privacy of the owner. Her clientele arrive by appointment and the gate discreetly swings open to admit their cars.

It is a beautiful yet unpretentious house with a somewhat chaotic interior created by the superimposition of numerous programmes. The geomancer visits every year as evidenced by the reflective mirrors which are visible in numerous locations in the house.

The interiors of the living areas were originally decorated with wallpaper from England and the United States with the exception of the library which had wood panels from 1977 onwards. However, the wallpaper deteriorated due to the humidity and so Patis Tesoro decided to experiment with trompe-l'oeils designed by her. She first started with the kitchen walls and other areas at the back of the living quarters which were divided into three sections and painted by three sets of muralists.

Above: The 2nd storey family room. The advice
of a geomancer is evidenced by the numerous
reflective mirrors.
Left: The living area. The walls are extensively
decorated with trompe l'oeil designed by
Patis Tesoro.

The first set of muralists was led by Benny Cabisada who was responsible
for the restoration of the paintings on the ceiling of San Augustin Church in
Intramuros (the Walled City of Spanish Manila) which is one of the oldest
surviving ecclesiastical structures in the Philippines. The second set of muralists
came from Pampanga, a province outside Metro Manila renowned for its artistic
talents. They painted the area where the family dines everyday, next to the
kitchen proper. The third section is the area nearest the hallway and used to be an
open space but was later incorporated into the kitchen area. This section was
painted by a former signage artist who started the work when he was in his 70s,
assisted by two apprentices. Unfortunately, he passed away and it has not been
possible to follow the geomancer's advice that a setting sun be added to the mural
to take advantage of the fire cycle.

The living room, patio and family room are all decorated with trompe-l'oeils
designed by Patis Tesoro and executed by Benny Cabisada.

The house is, like Jimmy Lim's House in Kuala Lumpur, a series of stage sets
upon which life is enacted. The structure has been added to and reconfigured on
several occasions since 1995 and the passage of time is conveyed in the juxtaposition of different activities. Residential life and work are almost totally entwined. Boundaries between the two are ambiguous though understood by the family
and their employees.

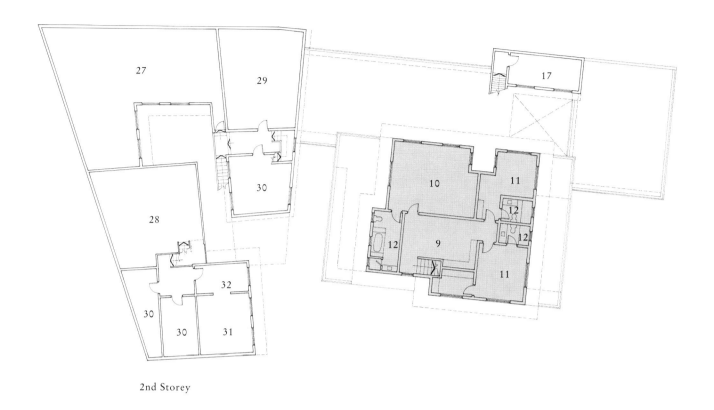

2nd Storey

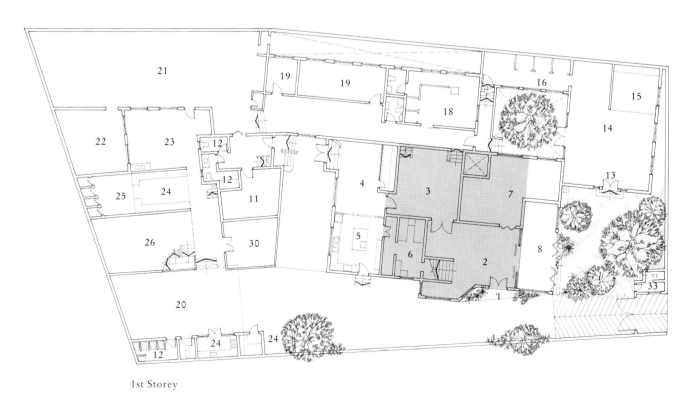

1st Storey

0 1   5   10m

1 entrance
2 living
3 formal dining
4 dining
5 kitchen
6 maid/linen
7 library
8 verandah
9 family hall
10 master bedroom
11 bedroom
12 bathroom
13 boutique entrance
14 boutique
15 cafe
16 fitting area
17 Patis Tesoro office
18 bridal room
19 office
20 garage
21 production area
22 embroidery room
23 laundry/drying area
24 employees kitchen
25 employees dining
26 employees bathroom
27 ladies quarters
28 mens quarters
29 KFF office
30 store
31 office
32 secretary

Fabrics and splendid bridal gowns are displayed in the boutique. The boundaries between residence and workplace are ambiguous.

The fitting room for bridal gowns.

FERNANDO HOUSE

The house is entered via a gravel drive and thence along a path of granite slabs set in grey pebbles.

When we had the house designed, my husband and I looked for an architect and found one in Lindy Locsin, who was young, very artistic and extremely imaginative. The house cost us then 32,000 pesos which is about the cost of a good sofa nowadays! **GILDA CORDERO-FERNANDO**

The Fernando House was built in 1958 to designs by Leandro V Locsin. Locsin was then a young practitioner who had come to prominence three years earlier with his design for the Chapel of the Holy Sacrifice. Later he would become the National Artist and the Philippines most venerated modern architect.

This was apparently the first family residence that he designed, a house with distinct Japanese imagery. The house is a long low-pitched timber-framed house. It has subsequently been extended on two occasions by the owner's daughter, architect Wendy Fernando Regalado. The two later extensions are sensitive to the spirit of the original house.

The Japanese influence is evident in the sliding screen walls and the proportions of the fenestration, in the slatted timber bridges which run around the house, in the external landscaping, and the manner in which the joints of the timber structural members are clearly articulated. The house is one room deep which facilitates cross ventilation. It is raised approximately 600 mm above the surrounding ground and this accommodates underfloor ventilation in the principle circulation spaces. It is a very cool house and at the heart of the plan is a landscaped courtyard which also facilitates cross ventilation and daylighting.

The house is entered from the street through a simple iron gate which gives access to a short, gravel drive. Leaving ones car in an open-sided car port, one proceeds via the gravel path, which crunches underfoot, before it changes to large granite paving slabs set in grey pebbles. Sensory experiences are subtly conveyed by these materials. The granite slabs lead to a narrow 'humped' timber bridge and the house entrance.

The scale of the house is not at all grand, indeed it is a modest, comfortable, almost 'bohemian' residence. It is imbued with the friendliness and artistic interests of its owners. Gilda Cordero-Fernando is a writer and publisher, her husband is a corporate lawyer. She is regarded as a cultural heroine of sorts and the house is becoming a living museum of modern art. Throughout the house

1 carport
2 entrance
3 study
4 dining
5 living
6 family
7 computor room
8 kitchen
9 utility
10 bedroom
11 bathroom/wc
12 guest room
13 storage (mezzanine over)
14 driver
15 maid
16 patio
17 pond
18 utility
19 water tank
20 3rd house (not shown)

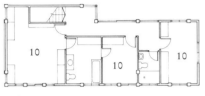

2nd Storey

Mezzanine

The granite path leads to a courtyard. The entrance to the house is over a 'humped' timber bridge.

0 1   5m

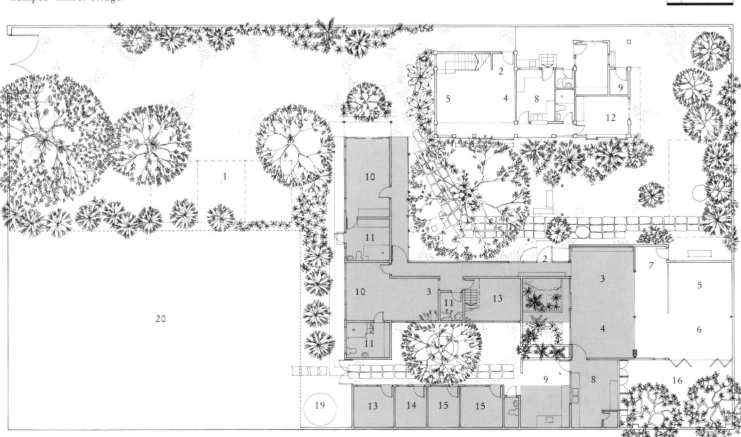

1st Storey

Above: The bedroom wing. The architectural language
has a distinct Japanese influence.
Right: The principle elevation faces the entrance court.
Sliding, glazed, timber-framed screens permit the house
to be naturally ventilated.

there are works by some of the Philippines foremost artists, indeed some have
been applied to the permanent structure.

Four striking black and white paintings by Onib Olmedo are hung in the
entrance corridor and alongside them a smaller black and white work by Bencab.
In the living room one encounters a papier-mache 'Dog with Cocked Leg' by
sculptor Roberto B Felio and a hardwood male nude by Jerusalino Araos. There
is a sensual lamp in the living room by the wildest of Philippines sculptors
Gabriel Barredo. Even the kitchen cabinets have been painted with a commen-
tary on the Philippines Spanish and American colonial periods by Karen Flores
while the guest room has a dramatic mural covering a whole wall entitled "Storey
Telling Time" by Elmer Borlongan.

One other artistic work, the tiled bathroom wall, contains all the debris of
family life: grandmothers miniature toys, little buddhas, old marbles, sea shells
gathered on children outings, bottles, and cracked seconds from a daughter-in-
laws kiln. These memories have been permanently embedded in a collage by
sculptor Roberto B Felio.

The house has in-between spaces where one is simultaneously inside and yet
outside. It relates to the garden: it encloses courtyards which are of an intimate
scale and which provide the setting for other sculptural works. In one courtyard
is a demonically twisted tree and by the entrance an orange *banca* (dug-out

canoe) recycled along with other 'found' material as sculpture by Henri Cainglet.

When Leandro Locsin designed the original house he placed it in one corner of the rectangular compound, a decision which at the time seemed rather odd to his clients but which they have come to respect the wisdom of. It permitted them to subsequently extend their house and to build two additional houses for their offspring in the remaining space.

Wendy Fernando Regalado has designed these two later houses in the family compound, for her brothers and their families. One, executed in association with Rosario Encarnacion Tan, is a remarkably simple modernist solution with high ceilings, that relates well to the original Locsin creation.

Above: Everyday Saints by Roberto B Fellio. The house is becoming a living museum of modern art.
Left: A high narrow corridor is the principal circulation route linking all parts of the house.

Books

Davidson, Cynthia (Editor).
Architecture beyond Architects,
AKAA, Academy Editions,1995.

Dumarçay, Jacques.
The House in South-East Asia,
Oxford, 1987.

Edwards, Norman.
*The Singapore House and
Residential Life 1819-1939*,
Oxford, 1990.

Jumsai, Sumet.
*Naga; Cultural Origins in Siam
and the West Pacific*,
Oxford, 1988.

Khan Hasan-Uddin.
Contemporary Asian Architects,
Taschen, 1996.

Klassen, Winand.
Architecture in the Philippines,
University of San Marcos,
Cebu, Philippines, 1986.

Kurokawa, Kisho.
*Intercultural Architecture:
The Philosophy of Symbiosis*,
Academy Editions, London, 1991.

Lee, Kip Lin.
The Singapore House,
Times Editions, Singapore, 1989.

Lim, William SW and
Tan, Hock Beng.
Contemporary Vernacular,
Select Books, Singapore, 1997.

Polites, Nicholas.
*The Architecture of Leandro
V Locsin*,
Weatherhill, Tokyo, 1977.

Powell, Robert. (editor)
Regionalism in Archiitecture,
Aga Khan Award for
Architecture, Concept Media,
Singapore, 1985.

Powell, Robert. (editor)
Architecture and Identity, Aga
Khan Award for Architecture,
Concept Media, Singapore, 1983.

Powell, Robert. (editor)
The Architecture of Housing, Aga
Khan Award for Architecture,
Geneva, Switzerland, 1990.

Powell, Robert.
The Asian House,
Select Books, Singapore, 1993.

Powell, Robert.
The Tropical Asian House,
Select Books, 1996

Powell, Robert.
*Line Edge and Shade: The Search
for a Design Language in Tropical
Asia*,
Page One Publishing,
Singapore, 1997.

Raman, PG. (editor)
*Criticism and Growth of
Architectural Ideas*,
Asia Forum, Singapore, 1993.

Ricoeur, Paul.
"Universal Civilisation and
National Cultures" in *History
and Truth*,
Evanston, 1966.

Rodrigo, D Perez III, Encarnacion,
Rosario S and Dacanay Jr., Julien E.
Folk Architecture,
GCF Books, Philippines, 1989.

Steele, James.
*Architecture for a Changing
World*,
Aga Khan Award for
Architecture, Academy Editions,
London, 1992.

Taylor, Brian Brace.
Geoffrey Bawa,
Concept Media, Singapore, 1986.

Taylor, Brian Brace.
MIMAR Houses,
Concept Media, Singapore, 1987.

Tettoni, Luca Invernizzi and
Sasrowardoyo, Tara.
Filipino Style,
Archipelago Press,
Singapore, 1997.

Tettoni, Luca Invernizzi and
Warren, William.
Thai Style,
Asia Books, Bangkok, 1988.

Tettoni, Luca Invernizzi.
Tropical Asian Style,
Periplus Editions, Singapore,
1997.

The Association of Siamese
Architects under Royal Patronage.
ASA profile,
Bangkok, Thailand, 1994.

Warren, William and Tettoni, Luca
Invernizzi.
The Tropical Garden,
Thames and Hudson,
London, 1991.

Zialcita, Fernando N and Tinio Jr.,
Martin I.
Philippine Ancestral Houses,
GCF Books, 1980.

Magazines and Journals

Singapore Architect,
No.195/97, Sep 1997.

Laras (Indonesia),
No.103, Jul 1997.

adobe (Filipino)
Soft volcanic rock found in the Philippines, brown in colour.

airwell (English)
A courtyard, open to the sky, which allows air and light to enter a building. A lightwell.

atap (Malay)
Roof thatch of woven palm leaves.

bahay kubo (Filipino)
The 'Philippine ancestral house', a *nipa* hut.

bahay na bato (Filipino)
A two storey house developed by the Spanish colonisers of the Philippines. It was a hybrid of the stone houses of the Mediterranean and the native *bahay kubo*.

clerestory window (English)
A high level window affording natural daylight.

Feng-shui or Fung-shui (Chinese)
Literally wind and water; a system of geomancy employed in China and elsewhere to bring practice into harmony with natural forces. It is used in determining the site or orientation of a city or a house. It is also used to determine the good or bad luck resulting from the siting in relation to cosmic elements.

five-foot way
In Sir Stamford Raffles proclamation to the Singapore Town Committee in 1822, it was stated that, "every house should have a verandah of a certain depth , open at all times as a continued and covered passage on each side of the street". Hence the five-foot way (six-foot way as was inserted in the clauses of all building leases at a later date).

kampong or kampung (Malay)
Village or settlement.
klong (Thai) Canal.

kopi tiam (Chinese)
Coffee shop, also a reference to a typical coffee shop table usually with marble top.

lanai (Filipino and Thai)
Open terrace.

Naga (Thai)
A water symbol which in Sanskrit means serpent.

nipa (Filipino)
A variety of palm, the leaves of which are used for thatching.

parti (French)
The initial design idea, the point of departure for a project.

patina (Latin)
A film or surface appearance that develops on wood or metal exposed to the elements.

sala (Thai)
Open-sided pavilion.

serambi (Malay)
Open verandah.

shophouse (English)
Shop with a dwelling above. Shophouses are usually built as a part of of a terrace, often with upper floors overhanging the first storey to form a covered pedestrian arcade. They were characteristic of the 19th and early 20th century commercial centres of Southeast Asian settlements.

soffit (English)
The underside of a beam.

terrace (English)
A platform adjoining a building usually used for leisure activities. An abbreviated expression for a terrace-house which is one of a row of houses sharing common party walls.

tromp l'oeil (French)
Something that deceives the eye, eg. a wall painting that has the appearance of reality.

tut-tut (Thai)
A three wheeled form of public conveyance usually powered by a (very noisy) two stroke engine.

venturi effect (English)
Induced movement of air through a building interior by the judicious or calculated placement of large and small apertures (windows, grills and roof openings etc.) in the external enveloppe.

verandah
A large open porch, usually roofed and partly enclosed by a railing, sometimes with the roof supported on pillars, often extending across the front and sides of a house.

AUTHOR'S NOTES

In Singapore the convention is to refer to the ground floor as the first storey. The upper floor of a two-storey house is referred to as the second storey. I have adopted this convention throughout.
All plans are accurate. In drawing the landscape I have relied upon photographs and site note. There may be inaccuracies in the exact position or in some cases the variety of tree depicted but the relationship is close to reality.